The Purposes of This Book

To Be a Resource for
any young man in his
teens or twenties who
wants to become a Man of Integrity
and Godly Character

and

To Be a Resource for
dads (or single moms, mentors, counselors,
or youth ministers) to
teach and train their teenaged sons
to become Men of Integrity and Godly Character
in accord with
Deuteronomy 6:5–9 and Ephesians 6:4

The Outcome

Reading and studying this book
should produce a young man
who is no longer a follower—a Sheep—
but has become a leader—a Shepherd!

A shepherd of great value
to his family, his community, and
to his nation.

Endorsements for *Sheep to Shepherd*

"In a world where many boys are growing up without the advantage of clear guidance, *Sheep to Shepherd* offers refreshing practical insight and instruction from a man who has led other men all his life. McDonald's crisp, insightful style causes the principles of this book to leap off the page and into the heart and mind."

—Dr. Allan Purdie
Pastor, Physician

"In his book, *Sheep to Shepherd*, with its focus on positive personal values and sterling character development, Tom McDonald has given us an important perspective on leadership. It is a great little book and I heartily endorse it for our young future leaders, parents, teachers, colleagues, employers, and anyone else concerned about the values that will guide our nation's future leadership."

—Dana G. Mead
Chairman Emeritus of the Massachusetts Institute of Technology
Retired Chairman and CEO of Tenneco, Inc.

"The State of our Union depends upon the strength and unity of our families—and that strength depends a lot on the presence, character, and leadership of fathers. I would like to put a copy of this book into the hands of every young man in America."

—Dr. Len Marrella
President, Center for Leadership and Ethics
Author of *In Search of Ethics*

"*Sheep to Shepherd* by Tom McDonald, like the cavalry to the rescue, stands up for virtues that make the male a man of integrity. It's a fast read, crammed with clear, frank, and engaging discussions that remind us what it takes to be a person of integrity and godly character."

—Robert Faulkender
Retired Army Officer, College Professor, Business Owner
Author of *Filtered By Time: A True Story of Success in Vietnam*

"This book, *Sheep to Shepherd*, is a must-read for leaders of young men, teachers, scout leaders, youth leaders, coaches, dads, and mentors of our young men. This message is vital for the future of America. We need young men to know how to lead with integrity and godly character."

—Denise Clark
Mother, Grandmother
Mentor to Women, Businesswoman, Entrepreneur

"Without following the principles of GOD and HIS WORD, it is nearly impossible for anyone to develop integrity in a world where the Truth has become relative and proponents of biblical standards are marginalized. If you are looking for a Bible-based model for training a young man or even a young person into a person of integrity, this fantastic book and the accompanying Study Guide are an effective tool to use. We are looking forward to using *Sheep to Shepherd*, in concert with the Bible, in transforming millions of young people throughout Africa."

—Dr. Ezra Aniebue
Chairman, African Pastors Network
www.africanpastorsnetwork.com

Sheep to Shepherd

Sheep to Shepherd

Tom McDonald

Alpharetta, Georgia

Copyright © 2012, 2017 by Thomas B. McDonald III
Third Edition
First Edition 2012

All rights reserved. No part of this book may be reproduced or transmitted in any form or by any means, electronic or mechanical, including photocopying, recording, or any information storage and retrieval system, without permission in writing from the publisher. For more information, address Heavenly Light Press, c/o Permissions Department, 1264 Old Alpharetta Rd., Alpharetta, GA 30005.

ISBN: 978-1-63183-097-6

Library of Congress Control Number: 2017903446

10 9 8 7 6 5 4   0 3 1 6 1 7

Printed in the United States of America

∞This paper meets the requirements of ANSI/NISO Z39.48-1992 (Permanence of Paper)

Unless otherwise indicated, Scripture is taken from the New American Standard Bible-Updated, copyright © 1960, 1962, 1963, 1968, 1971, 1972, 1975, 1977, 1995, 1997 by The Lockman Foundation. Used by permission.
Scripture quotations marked NLT are taken from the Holy Bible, New Living Translation, copyright © 1996, 2004. Used by permission of Tyndale House Publishers, Inc., Carol Stream, Illinois 60188. All rights reserved.
All word definitions are taken from the New World Dictionary of the American Language, 2nd College Edition, © 1980, Simon & Schuster (David B. Guralink, Editor in Chief).

For more information, please contact the author at Sheep2Shepherd@comcast.net or www.WordsAlongTheWay.com.

Contents

Acknowledgments	vii
Preface to the Third Edition	ix
Preface	xi
First Things First	1
Be Surrendered	7
Be Disciplined	13
Be Encouraging	21
Be Forgiving	25
Be Gentle	29
Be Honorable	33
Be Involved	39
Be Knowledgeable	43
Be Merciful	49
Be Prayerful	53
Be Respectful	59
Be Responsible	65
Be Tough Minded	69
Looking Ahead	73
Epilogue	87
Bibliography	97
Suggested Reading, Annotated	97
Study Guide	101

Acknowledgments

Heavenly Light Press is the first I must thank. Aspiring writers will be well served by this full-service professional self-publishing house. This young and dynamically led company of dedicated specialists is determined to greatly improve the image of self-publishing houses into one of high-quality competence and professionalism. Their printing setup is the latest in impressive high technology.

Then there were a few teens, some dads, and some of our church staff who encouraged me to go on from my talk to the boys and write the book. I also thank my pastor, Dr. Allan Purdie, who after reading it immediately asked me to teach it to all our high schoolers (Fall 2012).

A note of gratitude goes to Joe Hussung, our youth pastor, for his excellent idea for the chapter "Be Involved," as well as the idea to relate all the Behaviors to Jesus at the close of each chapter.

My warmest gratitude surely goes to my wife, Kay, an excellent proofreader and editor in her own right. She not only encouraged me along the way with good ideas in answer to my questions, but she also had some terrific ideas on organization of the book.

Preface to the Third Edition

The growing immorality and coarseness in the culture of twenty-first-century America are starkly reflected in the alarming decrease of personal integrity in public and private life, as well as in the increasing attacks, verbal and governmental, on the family and Christians. It is axiomatic that if the family is not producing young men (and women) of integrity and Godly character, then the culture and the nation begin to slide toward immorality, lawlessness, violence, and eventually anarchy.

To sustain a strong, morally healthy nation, God insists dads (the family Shepherd or leader) teach and train their sons (their Sheep) about the things of God and how to be men and leaders (Shepherds) before they leave home (Deut. 6:5–9, Eph. 6:4). Many of today's dads can't (or won't). No one can teach what he does not know. Those dads who do know, but are now not teaching such things, must be reinvigorated to engage in this essential task. Those who do not know will find this book invaluable for themselves as well. In short, we must restore and rebuild the family—the foundation of our culture and our nation.

The intent of this book, therefore, is to provide a resource to help dads teach their sons the minimum essential Behaviors they need to learn, embrace, and practice if they are to become mature men and responsible Citizens of Integrity and Godly Character. Pastors may want to reorient their youth and teen ministries to guide/teach dads and moms to be the primary teachers and mentors—while the church takes on a secondary/reinforcement role.

This book is for boys in their teens (and at-home young men in their twenties and thirties) **and their dads, single moms, or mentors to read and discuss together**. It presents twelve Behaviors that any male must make his own. The language and vocabulary make for easy reading. Its brevity eliminates the "daunt" factor.

The last chapter, "Looking Ahead," provides provocative yet insightful advice on five areas of life: Work, Higher Education, Marriage, Fatherhood, and Operating in the World. The book closes with a nugget-filled epilogue, a suggested reading list, and a complete study guide that help make it all stick.

Book "Happenings":
The founder of Abiding Word Ministries, a Biblical counseling ministry for adults and teens among seven churches north of Atlanta, has used this book in his work since 2013. He told the author that he had been looking for just this book for ten years. In mid-2015 he related that one of his teen counselees came to accept Christ as a result of reading this book.

A grandnephew (age fourteen) of the author took the book home after the 2015 Christmas visit and later told his grandmother that "it has completely changed my way of thinking."

The founder and chairman of the African Pastors' Network, after reading the book, asked the author to speak at his annual Atlanta Conference for Pastors in 2013. That video presentation, "Fixing a National Crisis," is on the author's website, www.WordsAlongTheWay.com.

Preface

Late in January of 2011, some men in my church asked me to bring a short talk for our young men as part of our first "Man Weekend." I was told there would be some thirty young men: half from middle school and half from senior high school. Furthermore, the purpose of the weekend was to teach the young men "man skills," such as fire building, knot tying, map reading, shooting, etc. I replied I'd be honored to bring the Saturday-evening message.

For the next week or so, I thought and prayed about what to say to these eager young men. I pulled out a number of the very fine books I've used over the years in mentoring men, with the thought that I would simply go through them to select a number of appropriate topics to talk about. I stacked up the books next to the pen and large yellow tablet on my desk. As I sat down to begin, I prayed for God's guidance.

I believe that God sovereignly gave me, out of my own experience of successes and failures, what you will read here. I have yet to look at the books, except to write the annotations for the suggested readings. After I completed the hurried but uninterrupted writing—it came off the end of my pen as fast as I could write—I read it all and it seemed to fit together as an excellent primer for Righteous Behavior in this world. *I understood that these are the things that*

God wants young men to know and practice to become the kind of men He can work with in this life.

I presented it to the young men that Saturday evening. They were transfixed in rapt attention. Some of the eight or so fathers and counselors who were there told me that they had never seen the boys sit so completely still and listen intently for that long, especially since they had all worked hard physically all day. *I can only conclude that these topics genuinely resonated with them and therefore would be useful to others their age (or maybe they were so tired they couldn't move).*

It strikes me that these Behavior Basics are not being taught or supported in the schools or, perhaps, not being discussed at home as much as they need to be. Therefore, I encourage using this primer for young men to help them along the way of becoming responsible and maturing as a man. *I am delighted to be able to come alongside the many dads, moms, or mentors out there who might use this to open a deeper dialogue with their sons on these and other topics.* I also recommend the books in the Suggested Reading section as good sources for additional discussion material.

Some of you may be wondering about my qualifications to talk about something as important as this broad topic of becoming a young Man of Integrity and Godly Character. Fair enough.

My story is simple: I was reared in a military family. Sorry to say, I was a rebel; I clashed with my father. I was not a good son. As a means to getting out of my house as fast as I could, I followed my father in attending the US Military Academy at West Point, New York. It was there that many of the lessons my father had tried to teach were hammered into me. Somehow I graduated, and had a twenty-six-year career in the military and served in leadership and command positions at several levels. As my career progressed, I found myself increasingly wanting to help young men escape the damaging clutches of a rebellious nature, by teaching them a winner's Behaviors toward becoming a leader among men.

Retiring as a colonel, I went to work in industry for three years. Not enjoying that, I started my own company and conducted business in the US and abroad for some nine years. I have been active as a servant leader in my local churches for over twenty years. I have worked with young and adult men of all levels of maturity and character in military service, the business world, academia, the community, and my local church. I think I have a good grasp of what Behaviors they need to know to thrive first as strong Sheep (instead of clueless, wandering Sheep) and later as Shepherds (leaders of Sheep).

Perhaps the most eventful aspect of my own journey on this earth was my accepting Jesus Christ as Lord and Savior at the "old" age of forty. He opened my eyes to see things as I had never seen them before. My own considerable failings have definitely honed my ability to see sin for what it is and what it does. It is a fundamental defiance of God and His better way, and it breaks His desired fellowship with us. My growing in His grace and knowledge enabled me to understand Behaviors of people in a whole new light. In my humble judgment, this changed life of mine as a leader and responsible man *with* God, after many years of knowing only *about* God, has given me a unique insight into what makes a "good" man and what makes a "godly" man. Sheep to Shepherd *is an opportunity to share my understandings with you in the hope that you, too, will see why each of us men needs to be a Man of Integrity and Godly Character.*

One final thing before we start. There is a much larger context underlying this topic of becoming a Man of Integrity and Godly Character. The men of the families of America determined the strength of the American family for centuries. These men taught the Behaviors in this book, and more, to their children. When the head of the family, a man, becomes weak and ineffectual in guiding, leading, and teaching in their home, then the family becomes weak and does not produce Men of Integrity and Godly Character. If the family—the bedrock of our culture, our society, our communities, and, therefore, our nation—is weak, then those institutions will become weak. This nation was established by our US Constitution from God through our Founding Fathers. The building block of our nation, the family, was firmly founded upon God Himself. God was our solid rock foundation. The accompanying diagram depicts in simplified form how our nation looked not too long after her founding.

A Nation Under God

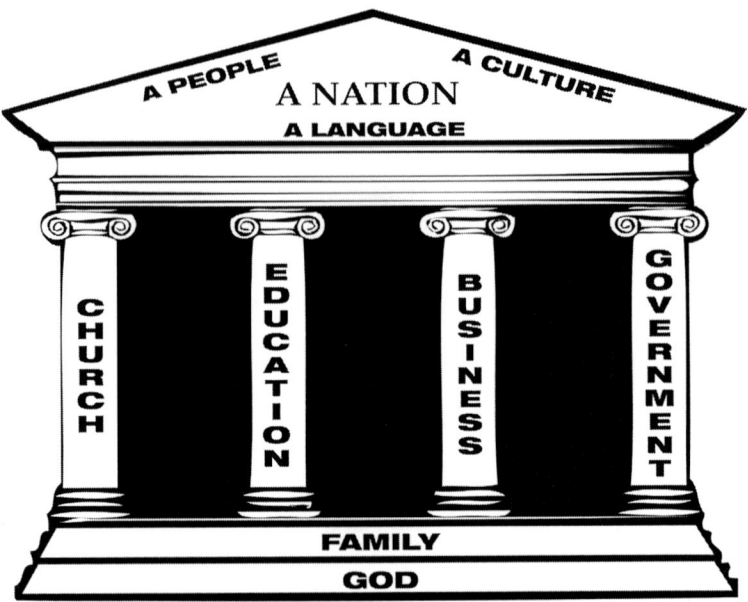

A People with their Culture and Language form a Nation. That Nation is supported, in the main, by the Pillars of Church, Education, Business, and Government. They all rest upon the Family from which all activities within any Nation spring. The Family, in turn, rests upon the strong and firm foundation of God Himself. Men of Integrity and Godly Character being raised in such families and later working in Church, Education, Business, and Government help keep the Pillars in balance with one another so that the fundamental structure of the Nation and its People and its Culture are not damaged. **A nation founded upon God, whose people worship Jesus, the Christ, enjoys Peace, Prosperity, and the Presence of God in ultimate victory.**

The next diagram depicts what happens when a nation gets out of balance and allows government to intrude corrosively into the lives of people (and the family) with no counterweight being provided by the Pillars of Business, Education, or the Church.

A Nation Under Idols

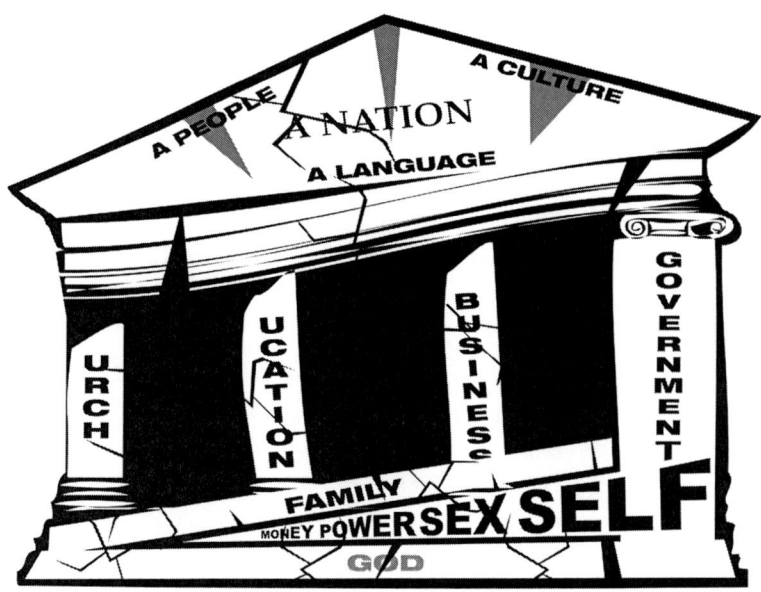

When the Pillars of Church, Education, and Business, begin to "allow" Government to intrude more and more deeply into the activities of Business, Education, and the Church, secularization begins to take place. People are enticed to turn away from the Church and God for their support and foundation. As people begin to depend upon the Government, they also begin to depend less on God. The Family is wedged loose from its moorings, its foundation upon God by the **idols** of money, power, sex, pride (self). When that happens, as it has in America, the men who are raised in the fracturing Family are more and more often NOT Men of Integrity and Godly Character. **A nation founded upon idols, whose people wallow in immorality, suffers Strife, Poverty, and the Presence of Evil in ultimate defeat!**

Look around you. Do you see our nation growing weaker morally, culturally, militarily, and in the level of respect that other nations around the world hold us? You can trace it to the weakening of the family—always. And that family weakening is directly due to the male head of household (if he is even present) not stepping up to his God-given responsibility to be the leader and Shepherd in his home in every way, especially in spiritual matters, and to teach these Behaviors and others to his children.

If the majority of the people of America want to again become a nation that glorifies God in all we say, think, or do, then we must begin now to rebuild the family from the inside out. The family Shepherd must raise his Sheep to become Shepherds, too. Anything short of that will, in my judgment, spell the end of America as we have known her, loved her, and for some of us, have been willing to die for her.

This book is only a part of that new beginning.

First Things First

Several years ago, God began sending men in their thirties and forties to me, a man in his midseventies. They asked to spend time with me—to mentor them to become more godly men. In the process, I have found that a truly godly man is one of whom the world is not worthy—men who can and will make a difference for God in this utterly lost world.

Some of my readings in 2011 revealed that when leaving home for college or work, "churched" young men also leave the church. Some aspects of the "feminist movement" have had a bad impact on what used to be the norm of young men maturing into solid men who can shoulder their manly responsibilities to lead our society. In an article in the *Washington Times* dated May 23, 2011, Mr. Willie Iles (National Director of Government Relations for the Boy Scouts of America) said the following:

> I am convinced today that we have a national crisis, a national security issue, a state of emergency issue and a nation at risk. If anybody cannot understand that, as we talk about investments and the return on those investments, which are our boys, then it is very clear we are going in the wrong direction.

Such insights from people who know about the state of our young boys are a great part of what has driven me to propose a different direction that must involve the teenage boy and his dad, mom, or mentor in the solution. *It's very clear that we must try to reach more young men before they become adult men out in the world earning a living.* But it may mean, too, that we may have to help some dads take on their God-directed responsibility toward their sons. *Mentoring men is a joy and a fruitful ministry, but there is a potentially more fruitful ministry awaiting those who would devote themselves to influencing young men in their twenties, in high school, or even younger.* This *can* be done in our churches, but it *must* be done in our homes. Public (government) schools many decades ago were an adjunct and extension to the home in teaching such matters, but with few exceptions, they now counter such teaching.

Of late, it has become my interest and special desire to help young men, especially teenagers, become godly young men, so that there is less difficulty in maturing into a Man of Integrity and Godly Character. The Bible is still true (and always will be) when it says that if we train up a child in the way he should go, when he grows old he will not depart from it (Prov. 22:6). God's Word about this is true, whether or not the way taught is wholesome. So it is crucial that we teach what *is* wholesome, true, righteous, and good so that godly character results. The younger we can teach this with true comprehension, the better the lasting impact for good—*on purpose and not by chance.*

Some things I've learned as I've journeyed toward maturing as a man:

- Being a man for God beats being a man for yourself.

- Better still is being a man who helps others become a man for God.

Let me ask you a few things: Does being a man mean knowing a lot of "man skills" like fire starting, map reading, shooting, knot tying, fishing, etc.? Is there anything wrong with learning these skills? Of course not—they are wholesome and needed skills. But, is there more to being a man than knowing these skills?

Doesn't what makes you who you are come from deep inside? What then are some of the basics that ought to guide your life as a man—from the inside out—from your **heart**?

And what is the "heart"? The dictionary says it is "The central, vital, or main part; real meaning; essence; core; one's innermost or hidden nature; fundamental being."

The Bible says, "Whatever is in your heart determines what you say" (Matt. 12:34b), and "Guard your heart above all else, for it determines the course of your life" (Prov. 4:23).

One last thing before we begin. If the purpose of this book is to help you along the way to become a Man of Integrity and Godly Character, we had better define those three words—"integrity," "character," and "godly"—just to make sure we are all on the same page.

Integrity is defined in *Webster's New World Dictionary*, 1980, as "the quality or state of being of sound moral principle; uprightness, honesty, and sincerity." So it would seem that integrity is a high and lofty goal; definitely worth the striving to attain it, wouldn't you say?!

Character is defined in the same dictionary as "moral strength; self-discipline, fortitude, etc." Some have said that our own character is best demonstrated to ourselves by how we act or behave when no one else is around or observing us. But we should not be content to be men of *just* good character, for that can be done through our own strength and will. Better that we aspire to be men of godly character, so let's define "godly."

Godly is defined in the same dictionary as "1) of or from God; divine. 2) devoted to God; pious; devout; religious."

Therefore, a man of Godly character is one whose moral strength is informed and disciplined by God's precepts and teachings in the Holy Bible, so as to live reverently, loyally, and obediently toward God.

In October of 2011, as reported in the November 2011 issue (vol. 40, no. 11) of *Imprimis* published by Hillsdale College, Michigan, an historian named Andrew Roberts was asked to speak at the dedication of a statue of Ronald Reagan at Hillsdale College. He began his address this way:

> The defining feature of Ronald Reagan was his moral courage. It takes tremendous moral courage to resist the overwhelming tide of received opinion and so-called expert wisdom and to say and do exactly the opposite. It could not have been pleasant for Reagan to be denounced as an ignorant cowboy, an extremist, a warmonger, a fascist, or worse by people who thought themselves intellectually superior to him. Yet Reagan responded to those brickbats with the cheery resolve that characterized not only the man, but his entire career. What is more, he

proceeded during his two terms as president to prove his critics completely wrong . . .

Oh, and did I mention, President Ronald Reagan was a strong Christian, too?!

If you are not yet a Christian yourself, we spend a bit of time on that topic in the next chapter, "Be Surrendered." Though this book is unapologetically biblical in its orientation, if you are not a Christian you will still be able to profit greatly from the teaching here. You will, trust me! It's just that if you are not yet a Christian, you will be unable to become the ultimate we are striving for here—to be a Man of Integrity and **Godly** Character. You can go through this book and adopt all that is here for you and become a man of integrity and **goodly** character—and there is nothing wrong and everything right with that. It's just that **Godly** character is the ultimate we are hoping to achieve for you, but certainly **goodly** is quite excellent and miles ahead of where most men are today.

To be a man of godly character, then, suggests we must behave always in all ways with all people as God would have us behave according to His Bible—and that we do so, not out of a sense of obedience, but out of our deep and growing love for Him.

Before we get started, let me bring up one more subject that is not discussed in detail in the book, but one that each of you has or should have a great deal of interest in. It is your life direction—your life dream. Do you have one? Have you thought about it? Have you talked about it with your dad or mom, or another trusted adult?

Life today moves much faster than it did when I was in high school. But even so, I had my life direction and dream mapped out in my junior year. So today, you should have your life direction or dream clearly laid out no later than that. If you are not there yet, you must spend some time thinking it through. Seek help from adults. Ask questions. Read about areas of work that interest you. Determine what makes you tick. What are you good at doing? What do you like to do?

One excellent resource for determining how God "wired" you (the talents and abilities you are born with) is found on the Career Direct website (www.careerdirectonline.org). Check it out, but whatever you do, waste no time in finding your life's direction.

One last helpful thought before you start: **Please take time now to read the introduction to the Study Guide on pages 101 and 102** . . . and then follow its suggestions to get the most out of your effort here.

Okay then, let's get started!

Be Surrendered

All the Behaviors in this book are in alphabetical order but this one, which is more of a transaction. Why is that? Why would "Be Surrendered" be the first? Could it be that all else is subordinate to this one transaction? *Could it be that the decision to accept Jesus Christ, the Son of God (sacrificed to pay the penalty for my sin and your sin) as your Savior and Lord, is the single most important decision you will ever make in all your life here on earth?!* And can it be that all else in life cannot be seen as God sees it unless we have His Holy Spirit in us through acceptance of Jesus—to guide us—to give us His eyes?

In the Bible, this surrender is referred to as being saved. From what are we to be saved? Why do we need saving?

It all began in the Garden of Eden with Adam and Eve at the beginning of the earth and all of creation. After God explicitly told them not to eat of the Tree of the Knowledge of Good and Evil, they did so after being tricked by Satan. As punishment for their disobedience, called sin, God banished them from the Garden of Eden, lest they eat of the Tree of Life and live forever in their fallen (sinful) state. Another huge thing that resulted is that God took His Holy Spirit from them and they died spiritually, not physically. (Remember,

God told them they would die if they ate the forbidden fruit? Well, they did die—spiritually!)

Sin, therefore, carries huge consequences. Sin separates us from God. Sin means doing what's wrong in God's sight. He gave us the Ten Commandments to show us the basics of what to do and what not to do. So, if you've ever lied, stolen, cheated on a test, disobeyed your mother or father, longed for "stuff" someone else had, not loved or followed God, and not treated other people as you would like to be treated—well then, you've sinned. We are all born sinners, because it is not in our nature to keep the Law of God.

Is there a way back to God? Yes! God Himself provides it. It is called Salvation or being saved. The Bible has quite a bit to say about being saved. "For God did not send the Son into the world to judge the world, but that the world should be saved through Him" (John 3:17). "And if it is with difficulty that the righteous is saved, what will become of the godless man and the sinner?" (1 Peter 4:18). "For God so loved the world that He gave His only begotten Son, that whoever believes in Him shall not perish, but have eternal life" (John 3:16). Never forget this: *We are not human beings on a spiritual journey; we are spiritual beings on a human journey.*

Incidentally, you may have heard someone say that there are many ways to God. But God the Son said in His Word, "I am the Way, the Truth, and the Life; no man comes to the Father except through Me" (John 14:6). You can argue this point, but it would be foolishness, because Jesus proved He was God the Son by dying on a Roman Cross, being resurrected by God His Father, and being seen by hundreds of witnesses whose testimonies are recorded in the Bible and in other books of history written in that time. After that He ascended into Heaven, watched by many witnesses, to await the day when He will return to earth for His faithful. I want you to be among those faithful.

So there is only one transaction in all of life that can save you and assure you or any of us of going to live with God when you're finished here on earth. That transaction involves admitting that you are a sinner (as each of us is) and believing that Jesus is God's Son who died for that sin. Then, ask Jesus to forgive you and become your Savior and Lord. If you do this from your heart, you will be saved! Saved from going to Hell when you die, and guaranteed to go to Heaven to be with God. In fact, it is being with God that makes it the Joy of Heaven—just as not being with God makes it the torment of Hell. Think of it this way: if you're saved, this life is the only Hell you'll ever know; if you're not saved, this life is the only Heaven you'll ever know. As a Christian, this is not your home; you're just traveling through en route to Home!

There is more that you should know about this essential transaction with our Creator God. And that is that He will not only forgive your sin, but He will, if you let Him, take the old things of your life away, and all things in your life will be made as though new. But perhaps the most wonderful part of this whole affair is that He will give you His Holy Spirit, who was taken from Adam and Eve, as you may recall from our earlier words! The Holy Spirit will be your personal guide through all of life. He will comfort you, guide you, and teach you the things of the Bible as you read it.

If you have never trusted your life to Christ Jesus, go ahead and take the time now to stand before our Creator God, make your confession of sinfulness, repent from your life of sinfulness, accept His forgiveness, and welcome Jesus Christ as your Lord and Savior in this new life with and for Him. "For He [God, the Father] rescued you from the domain of darkness, and transferred us [you] to the kingdom of His beloved Son, in whom we have redemption, the forgiveness of sins" (Col. 1:13,14). To God alone be the Glory!

And you will most certainly want to share the wonderful good news of your salvation with others. And that is one of the many things the Holy Spirit does for you; He gives you a joy about His having taken up residence in you so that you sometimes are fairly bursting to tell others about Him. Go ahead, this Good News is contagious! You will develop a hunger and thirst for learning more about God from His Bible, so *do it*.

Join a Christ-centered, Bible-preaching/teaching church and begin your growth as a Christian. You can accelerate your growth as a follower of Christ Jesus by asking an older Christian man (how 'bout your dad?) to disciple you—to mentor you. Some of the books in the Suggested Reading list at the end of the book can be used for discipling you. One of the best and most comprehensive discipling helps is Design for Discipleship from navpress.com. So select your mentor and get started.

Now, you may see why I put this transaction as the first Behavior that you should "make your own." One of the great verses in the Bible is in Matthew 6:33, "But seek first His kingdom and His righteousness, and all these things will be added to you." Without God's Holy Spirit guiding and directing your life, you may have much unnecessary difficulty in your life, and it will make Becoming a Man of Integrity and Godly Character impossible.

If you are not ready at this time to surrender your life to Jesus, then know this: All the teachings in this book are very much needed by all of us men, whether one is a Christian or not. So read on, but know, too, that you can only become a man of integrity and *goodly* character, not *godly* character, without Jesus. If you want to be the best you can be for God, then come to Christ Jesus as soon as you will. Keep this in mind: *the surrender to Jesus is the only total surrender in which there is total victory!*

Be Disciplined

The Webster 1980 dictionary says that discipline is "The result of training that develops self-control, character, or orderliness and efficiency."

Another insight that we should not miss is that the words discipline and disciple have the same root. Perhaps you have heard that the name for the group of men who followed Jesus and listened and learned from His teaching were "disciples"—the twelve disciples. To be a disciple is to follow and learn from the leader and teacher. That suggests that a disciple must discipline himself to listen (or read) in order to learn.

But the word also carries the very strong meaning of self-control. A new recruit in the army is put through a rigorous physical, mental, and emotional time of testing and training right at the beginning of his time in the army. He has strong discipline imposed upon him by his drill instructor for the purpose of teaching the new recruit how he should act (behave) in the army under all sorts of situations. And after a time of intensive learning, the recruit becomes a soldier who is able to carry on these same disciplines within himself without the DI having to impose them.

The soldier is then said to be self-disciplined; he is self-controlled. That is a very important part of becoming a man, as well as a soldier. To be worth anything to himself and others, like his employer, a man must be self-controlled; he must be self-disciplined. As an example, you will need to discipline yourself to learn all the Behaviors in this little book for young men. Doing so will pay you large dividends throughout your life.

What, then, are some of those things you should learn to be a self-disciplined Man of Integrity and Godly Character?

Purity

Let's start by going immediately to an element of maturity and self-discipline that is tough for most young men in today's culture. That is the concept of sexual purity. God makes it abundantly clear in His Word that we are not to engage in sexual intercourse until we are married—and then, only with one's wife. Anything else is way outside God's will for us (God calls it sin).

It is like shooting an arrow at a target and hitting anything other than the center of the bull's-eye, which is missing the mark of perfection. In the same manner, if we do not live as God has told us to live, we have missed the mark of His perfection—which is, you guessed it, sin. Our culture today is soaked in sex and sexual images. Watching the ads on TV, you can't even sell paint without a sexy model enticing you to buy. It's sick and immature, but that is what our pleasure-seeking society has done to itself. Do not fall for the tricks of the devil in this age of "anything goes." It doesn't "go" in God's view of things. He designed His most wonderful gift of sex to be enjoyed only in a holy marriage. If you violate that, there are untold consequences: unwanted pregnancy, abortion, disease, diminishing the joy of the act that God had planned for you to have in marriage, etc. Just don't do it. Keep yourself pure until you are married, and even then, don't stray; stay pure! And do not go near pornography; it is addictive and can ruin you!

Your genitalia make you a male, not a man. Your disciplined mind and heart are what will make you a man! So you must make a conscious, sober decision to become a man, and then do all in your considerable power, with God's help, to be a man—His man, 24/7/365. So do it!

Sober

Another aspect of the society around us today that can appeal to young men is a trap. And that is the appeal of not growing up. Remaining immature, even childish—maybe even "escaping" the rigors of real life through drugs—exemplifies the ultimate coward. An immature person does not care to take up the responsibilities of manhood, to get an education, to leave home to make his own way in life, to become competent in some field of endeavor, to be of service to his community, to help others come along, to raise responsible children to become mature adults, to choose the harder right in life rather than the easier wrong, to become a Man of Integrity and Godly Character.

Today, we have unmanly adults staying at home and not going out to start their own lives. We have men who refuse to be of sober spirit and stalwart character. In effect, they want to remain children, wimpy "men," who would not even think to take up arms to defend their country if asked. Now I am not talking about a young man, a son, who runs into some sort of financial reverse after once having left home to make his way. There will be times like that, but they must be short times given over to rethinking your way forward, regrouping your assets, and making a new start—and leaving home once again.

Focused

A camera lens must have the ability to bring the rays of light from a scene together in such a way that they project a miniature of the image of the scene onto the film or recording plate. If the lens is not made in a disciplined manner to be perfect, the image will not be sharp; it will be out of focus, it will be fuzzy. Likewise, if you are not disciplined and focused in your thinking as you go through life learning all that it has to teach you, your "picture" will be distorted and fuzzy. You must remain focused to learn, and that takes, you guessed it, discipline. Most of us who enjoy life enjoy it because there are so many excellent things to learn in God's magnificent creation. Those who most enjoy their journey through life discipline themselves to remain focused—to draw from what is all around them—to include establishing and enjoying great relationships.

Committed

Perhaps one of the more difficult concepts to understand and to practice is the idea of being committed—to God, of course. The "world" will ridicule such an idea. The world will try to teach you to commit to no one, to be true only to yourself, to be in control, to "do it my way," etc. Self-centeredness is what the world preaches, or, alternatively, it will suggest you give yourself away to Gaia, the earth goddess, or to some other unworthy cause. One of the most prevalent "alternative commitments" is to drugs or alcohol (actually a drug, too); it is a dead-end street—sometimes literally. There is a very definite "expiration date" to this lifestyle. Do not even get started with a trial or test of the stuff. If you are one of those who is susceptible to addictions (and you may not know that until too late), it will suck you in and most probably ruin your life. All for a momentary "high." Just plain dangerous. Any or all of these are a devil's tool to keep you from giving yourself to the God of Creation, because most of the people of this world refuse to say He is God, or to admit Jesus is Lord. They are utterly lost in a web of their own deceit and want you to come be part of their hopeless situation. "Submit therefore to God. Resist the devil and he will flee from you" (James 4:7). There is much more on this in the chapter "Be Surrendered."

And what does this commitment to God look like? How do you do that? It is actually quite simple. Just tell God every day, from the bottom of your heart, that you want Him to lead you every step of the way that day. Some people get up a bit earlier every day to spend time with the Lord with some prayer, some Bible reading, and some quiet time to just sit before Him and praise Him for Who He is. You can read some chapters from the Bible, and/or you can pray to Him about issues in your life where you need His help. One excellent online site for a daily Bible verse and lesson is from Moody Bible Institute; it is www.todayintheword.com.

You will grow in spiritual strength if you practice such a "Quiet Time" each day. It doesn't have to be a long time, maybe five or ten minutes at first. He will guide you into a longer, deeper time with Him as He thinks you're ready. Just enjoy Him and worship Him—for He is surely worth it, wouldn't you say?! After a while you will find that you miss the strength and comfort that such a time gives you when you occasionally miss a day or two, as all of us do from time to time.

Self-Starter

This old world is full of people who would rather just quit on themselves and others. The going gets a little tough, so they just sit down in place and quit. It happens with educated people, with talented people, with really smart people. They don't have the persistence or determination to carry on, to "git 'er dun," as we say in the South. Young men must recapture the idea that they are responsible for their future (hopefully in partnership with God), not their parents. Getting out of the house and getting on with your life should be the normal, healthy desire of every red-blooded American boy and young man. Anything less brands you as a parasite, someone who lives off another. How sad. Don't let this be you. Become determined in your approach to your life; be persistent; get some "fire in the belly." Take a look at Proverbs 28:19 for another perspective on this.

Physical Condition

Obesity is often a clear indicator of a lapse of self-discipline. Just as a terribly underweight person indicates a potential serious malady, obesity is known to cause medical problems, especially in later life. But even young people who are heavy (fat) contend with many issues that affect their ability to work and live. Good dietary/nutritional habits, all well known, are essential to staying sharp physically. Another aspect of this healthy lifestyle is exercise; a good rule of thumb is walk or run five days a week for a minimum of twenty minutes each day, and do a vigorous strength-training workout three times a week. You need to rest your body properly, too. Teens need more sleep because their bodies are going through a huge transition from boy to man in the adolescent years. You should aim for a full eight hours of sleep a day every day, say from 10 p.m. to 6 a.m. Oh, stop grumbling; it's for your own good both now and long term.

Jesus is our example for discipline. In fact, His entire life was one of complete discipline to the will of His Father. He prayed often and long. He taught the ideas, principles, and concepts given Him by His Father. And finally, in total discipline, He went to the cross to die agonizingly so that we all could live forever with Him after we leave earth—if we so choose.

Here is something on the next page worth your thought and contemplation, called "Press On," by Calvin Coolidge and modified in the last phrase by the author. Make a copy of it and frame it and hang it on the wall next to where you study or work.

I submit to you that if you take this powerful encouragement to heart, it will lead you to have godly *character* and steadfast *integrity*—and all to the Glory of God!

PRESS ON

Nothing in the world can take
the place of PERSISTENCE.

Talent will not.
Nothing is more common than
unsuccessful men with talent.

Genius will not.
Unrewarded genius
is almost a proverb.

Education alone will not.
The world is
full of educated derelicts.

PERSISTENCE and DETERMINATION
alone are omnipotent.

And if EXCELLENCE is to attend your RESULTS,
Then surrender your LIFE to the
LORD of HEAVEN and EARTH!

And PRESS ON—*with* Him!

Be Encouraging

Can you think of someone who is an encourager? One of the sure signs to identify such a person is that you feel good about yourself after having been in his presence for a while. And why is that? Well, usually they are people who are upbeat, positive, and enjoy life. But there is another characteristic that is sure to be present: they are interested in you more than they are interested in themselves. They want to know what you're up to, what your interests are, and how you're doing. They spur you on to accomplish any goals that you may have shared with them. By their questions and conversation, they let you know that you are valued. Such a person makes us feel good and even gives us some motivation to go on and do better.

Let's define "encouragement." It means "giving courage, hope, or confidence." The Bible speaks of being an encourager in several places. One of my favorites is in 1 Thessalonians 5:11, "Therefore encourage one another and build up one another, just as you also are doing." Another is in Hebrews 10:23–25:

> Let us hold fast the confession of our hope without wavering, for He who promised is faithful; and let us consider how to stimulate one another to love and good deeds, not forsaking our own

assembling together, as is the habit of some, but encouraging one another; and all the more as you see the day drawing near.

You can be one of those people. You can be an encourager. The Bible talks of Barnabas (whose real name was Joseph), a name that means "son of encouragement." He was the first to befriend Paul after Paul's conversion and three-year Arabian-wilderness experience, and then introduced him to the other apostles. He convinced them that Paul was no longer behaving as the Pharisee named Saul of Tarsus, who angrily persecuted the early Christians. He encouraged them all to accept Paul as a true apostle, one who had been trained personally by Jesus. Sometime you may have to do something as dramatic as Barnabas did, so be prepared.

And how do you prepare yourself? Develop an attitude of being on the lookout for people who need a lift. All of us should seek to lift the hearts of those who are downcast around us. This life is a downer for more people than you might imagine. So watch for opportunities to be an exhorter like Barnabas. Such people, by the way, are never without friends, because people just simply like to be around positive and encouraging people.

One final thing about this encourager role: as the Holy Spirit leads, inspire others to come up higher. Positive people are often asked why they are so upbeat all the time. This provides you an easy opportunity to tell them about your Lord and Savior, Jesus the Christ, and how He changed your life. They, too, can come up higher if only they will confess, repent, surrender, and ask Jesus to be their Lord. Now that's higher!

Tom McDonald

Jesus was a constant Encourager. Just before His ascension, He gave us the Great Commission (Matt. 28:18–20). At the end of His "commissioning" of us all, He encouraged us by saying, "I am with you always, even to the end of the age."

Be Forgiving

This may be another of the more difficult Behaviors for a person to master, but it does not have to be.

Let's first look at what the dictionary has to say about this. "One who forgives, gives up all claim to punish or exact penalty for an offense; overlook; to cancel a debt; to give up resentment against; to stop being angry with; pardon." That's a tall order.

Can you forgive all hurt immediately? Few of us can. But we must eventually; the sooner the better. And when you do, can you "let it go" so that you don't think about it ever again? It is virtually impossible for us humans to forget a wrong done to us, but we should at least put it as far back in our minds as we can. Likewise, do you seek forgiveness from those you have hurt? That's why I say this may be one of the toughest Behaviors to master. Let's talk about all this . . .

If someone you love hurts you unintentionally, is it easier to forgive him or her than it is to forgive the same offense from an acquaintance or stranger? Probably yes, right? So what is the difference between these two events? Love. Love is the difference. If we love someone, we usually want to forgive them. But the Bible says that we are to love our neighbors as we love ourselves. And later on, that same

Bible says that we who believe in Jesus as Lord are to love one another as Jesus loves us—which is, He loved us enough to die for us. So that is a much higher order of love and much harder to achieve. Taking both of those together, it means that God wants us to behave toward all strangers (our "neighbors"), friends, and all Christians the same way when they have hurt us, intentionally or unintentionally; *we are to forgive them*. By forgiving them, we are displaying God's kind of love.

He came to earth as a man to show us how to live a life of love—to be like Him. So we better examine what exactly characterizes a "life of love." Very simply God defined it by the single most amazing act of Love the World has ever experienced. You've all heard it said and have even seen flash signs of "John 3:16" held aloft by spectators at televised sports events. It says that God *gave* His Son to be a sacrifice to pay our penalty for all our sins so that He could *forgive* all of us who will believe in Him. So that is the sum total and fullest meaning of LOVE as God sees it. He *gave* and *forgave*. We are to love others as He loves us—forgiving any who wrong us. That is LOVE.

How are you doing with this business of forgiving? Do you prefer to carry a grudge? Do you want someone to be punished for what you perceive they have done to you? Or do you want to do things God's way—forgive them as soon as you are able (with the Holy Spirit's help) and really mean it? Have you ever thought about the scary words from Jesus recorded in Matthew 6:14–15? He said, after He had just finished teaching his disciples to pray, "If you forgive those who sin against you, your heavenly Father will forgive you. But if you refuse to forgive others, your Father will not forgive your sins" (NLT). Did you get that?

That's precisely how seriously God Himself thinks about this FORGIVENESS business. In short, God allowed His Son to be brutally sacrificed so you can have a "get-to-Heaven-free card." If you turn around and do not forgive some other human being their sin against you, He will take a dim view of your inability to LOVE as He has LOVED you. That dim view is played out by Him *not* covering you with His Grace. See Matthew 18:23–35. Think about verse 35.

Let me tell you from my own experience what happens by *not forgiving*. If I do not forgive but instead carry the hurt and anger around in me, I am the one ultimately hurt because it can cause me to have an internal physical or emotional breakdown of some sort: an ulcer in the stomach, a sour attitude toward life, an inability to be a proper witness for Christ. So don't go there. Forgive and, as best you can, forget it and get on with your life.

If you harbor *unforgiveness* in your heart toward anyone, you are making a mockery of your salvation and casting serious doubt on your being a son of God—which, of course, ruins your witness to others about the saving Grace of God Almighty. He wants us all to pass it on. LOVE everyone by both *giving to* and *forgiving* them.

Are "I'm sorry" and "Please, forgive me" different? You bet they are. Anyone can say they're sorry and it can mean a whole bunch of things, none of which come close to asking forgiveness. If you humble yourself to someone to ask them to forgive you for a hurt against them, you are doing what God wants you to do. And it is the only way to bury the hurt to restore the relationship. And that, my young friend, is what Life in Christ ultimately is all about—*restoring relationships*.

Let's cover a few last-minute things that are no less important than the others. Are we to be forgiving toward our saved friends only? Nope! God says to forgive all; that means saved, lost, or even enemies.[1] And we are to pray for all. As best we are able—and we are able in Him—be Peacemakers. Bottom line, as we have said earlier, is that your manner and behavior must honor Christ in all you *say, think, or do.* Anything short of that will not point other men to Him.

So let's love like Christ. One way to do that is to live the Golden Rule[2] in all your dealings with others. There is one more thing, however. We are to hate all sin, all evil, yet He asks us to pray for chronic evildoers. God's love is a special kind of love. And what is that special kind of love? In the Bible it is the Greek word agape. It means "unconditional love," the kind of love Jesus showered on us to pay for our sins, for our "hurting" Him. The only way you and I will ever "get it" is to live it. The greatest measure of our love for others is how we handle the issue of forgiveness. Jesus is our ultimate example of forgiveness; He gave all on the cross for us and told us how to love[3] others.

---

[1] Matt. 5:44 "But I say to you, love your enemies and pray for those who persecute you."
[2] Luke 6:31 "Treat others the same way you want them to treat you."
[3] John 15:12 "This is My commandment, that you love one another, just as I have loved you."

Be Gentle

You're probably saying to yourself something like, "What do you mean 'be gentle'? I'm going to be a man, and men aren't gentle." Is that true? Is it better, then, for a man to be violent, rough, harsh, or severe, which are the opposites of gentle? How about the synonym for gentle of "peaceable"? Okay, we can go with that, but at least I got you thinking about the whole idea of this sort of Behavior. After all, who is to be our model for this Behavior? Can't do any better than model the "Prince of Peace," right?

And what did Jesus say about this to His disciples while teaching them on the Mount of Olives? The third so-called Beatitude is "Blessed are the **gentle**, for they shall inherit the earth" (Matt. 5:5). The *MacArthur Study Bible* says this in the notes for this verse: "Gentleness or meekness is the opposite of being out of control. It is not weakness, but supreme self-control empowered by the Spirit."

Some Bible translations render the word "gentle" as "meek," a similar word to gentle. Some have said that "meek" is "strength under control." I would say to you that a true man of God is meek only when his strength is under God's control. So being meek or gentle is something that God wants to see in His people, men and women. There is a pithy quote to help you to remember to be gentle in all your dealings with others: "You can't grow roses with a hand grenade!"

We have mentioned the Beatitudes here, and this is as good a time as any to tell you that is precisely why I am calling the several items of personal conduct in this book the Behaviors—they all flow out of the Beatitudes. No man can ever improve upon what God in Jesus has already given us, but we can adapt it to further use, as we do here, for your good.

Let's face it, if you curb your anger, absorb insults, and are slow to speak (and then, softly) people will see you to be a person of restraint, of self-control, one who is disciplined. One who is able to control his temper, to be in control of himself, draws people to him. The opposite display of behavior repels people. No one really wants to be around a loose cannon or someone who can't control his temper. Remember the Golden Rule we just covered in the last chapter, "Treat others the same way you want them to treat you." We should all treat others the way that we want to be treated, just as Christ did when He was on the earth.

In all the Gospel reports about Jesus, He is, with two exceptions, a very meek and gentle man. Those two exceptions are when (at the front and near the end of His earthly ministry) He drove the moneychangers and animal sellers out of the temple courtyard. And that violence was caused by their profaning His Father's house of Prayer with worldly (and possibly corrupt) commerce. This example of Jesus's ungentle behavior shows us that there is a time for ungentle behavior, but only when it is in pursuit of a righteous objective or there is a violent, bad situation needing urgent and forceful intervention. For the greater part of your life and mine, we should be gentle in all our dealings with the world around us. One last thought here: no one, including a Christian, is called to be a doormat for others. As best you can, in such situations, turn aside the attempt gently. Gentleness is winsome; harshness is not.

Be Honorable

This Behavior, Be Honorable, is not that difficult to grasp or understand, but for some it may be very difficult to practice. We'll cover why that is a bit later, but first let's get a good working understanding of the word "honorable." The dictionary says that honorable means "having or showing a sense of right and wrong; characterized by honesty and integrity."

Scripture says quite a bit about honor and honorable. In Philippians 4:8, it says, "Finally, brethren, whatever is true, **whatever is honorable**, whatever is right, whatever is pure, whatever is lovely, whatever is of good repute, if there is any excellence and if anything [is] worthy of praise, dwell on these things." Then Proverbs 29:23 says, "A man's pride will bring him low, but a humble spirit will obtain **honor**." These two, taken together, suggest that to become a man of honor, one must first be humble before God and man, and do all things which are right, true, pure, and lovely and do them with excellence—to the glory of God.

We have all seen men who are humble, though strong, and they always seem to do things very well—with excellence. We naturally tend to honor that man, to think highly of him because he does all things well without any hint of ego, pride, or bragging. They just seem to be great people to be around. For example, these are the men who will never be untruthful, never cheat on an examination, and who will never keep the wrong change some cashier gave them in the checkout line. It's the kind of person who just wants to do the right thing for the right reason—all the time.

There is something else about that kind of person, too. He also appears interested in us—in what we are about, and what we are doing. He is always ready to give you a helping hand and to give sound advice humbly (without lording it over you as though he's the hotshot and you're not). We are attracted to men like that. They may not be leaders, per se, but they just seem to make us want to be better than we are. And if we spend enough time around them, we begin to take on those same characteristics. We become humble and are ready and willing to help others achieve what they need to achieve. We become men who "never settle for a half truth when the whole can be won" (quote from the Cadet Prayer from the United States Military Academy, West Point, New York).

Let me make it very clear to you what honorable is by showing you its opposite. A man who is dishonorable is one who is not trusted in anything he does or says, because he has become known to be a liar, a cheat, and/or a thief. The Bible talks about the one who comes to steal, kill, and destroy—and elsewhere is referred to as the "father of lies." And who is that? Yes, the devil himself. The essence of evil. So you see, don't you, that if you decide to engage in lying, or cheating, or stealing, you are in league with the devil, the most evil creature in all of the universe. That is NOT where someone who intends to be a Man of Integrity and Godly Character should go—not even once—not even a little. There is no such thing as a little lie, or a little cheating, or a little stealing. Do not go there—ever. If you have, then get it cleaned up with God right now. Confess it to Him, repent of it, and then ask Jesus to forgive you—He will, instantly. Then resolve that, with His help, you will Be Honorable from that point on.

Another aspect of being honorable is being straight up with all men, all people, all the time. There will be no fakery, no phoniness in us. At a minimum it means being absolutely honest in all our dealings with all mankind.

For an honorable man, when stray, tempting ideas about lying, cheating, or stealing come into his mind, he will not "entertain" them, but immediately quash them and banish them from his mind. This kind of temptation comes not from God, but from the world, the devil, and even your own flesh, your own mind.

One of the best scriptures in the Bible for dealing with this sort of attack is found in the book of James 4:7. It says, "Submit therefore to God. Resist the devil, and he will flee from you." When you are tempted, just say to your flesh or the devil, "I stand against you, I resist you. Now go away as scripture says you will." To tell you the truth, that is one of the best ways to use the Sword of the Spirit (one of the names for the Holy Bible). And if you have some of these great warrior scriptures memorized, you can unsheathe your own memorized sword and use it against all manner of evil at the right time. That's one very practical reason for memorizing scripture as part of your Bible-study routine.

Being honorable in life is also important if you want to be perceived as credible. Can people really trust you? If you are an honorable young man, people, over time, will notice that you are—and from that point on, unless you go bad, you will be believed in all you say or do. You will be recognized as an honorable man. That's a great place to be, so that your word becomes your bond. If you say it, it is so.

The United States has several military academies and each of them has an honor code. The honor code at West Point (the United States Military Academy) says, "A Cadet will not lie, cheat or steal, or tolerate those who do." That sort of honor inculcation is essential to forming honorable men as cadets, because, upon graduation, cadets are commissioned as military officers in the army. I think you can see that in the military it is crucial that each officer be able to trust absolutely what another officer communicates to him. Lives may depend upon the truthfulness of a report, in war or peace. In fact, to continue this theme of being honorable in all things, the motto of West Point and her graduates is "Duty, Honor, Country." This motto, or pledge, guides each of them for the rest of their lives.

I want to share a story about General Creighton Abrams, the army chief of staff after whom the awe-inspiring M-1 Abrams main battle tank was named. He was a brilliant, but crusty, veteran of much combat. One day, as the story goes, he was talking with some of his general staff officers in the Pentagon and the subject got around to the army officer corps and the need to ensure that policy made in the Pentagon not "take away from an Officer his Honor." Hearing that, General Abrams stood to his feet and gruffly looked around the room, looking at each face intently, as he said, "No man EVER has his honor taken from him; he can only give it up. It cannot be taken from him—ever. Do I make myself clear?" And sat down. The general was right on. Your honor cannot be taken from you; you must give it up yourself.

We really should not leave the Behavior of Be Honorable without at least briefly discussing ethics and morality. Why? Because ethics support and inform your decision to be honorable. You can't be honorable and unethical, for example.

Let's first define ethics: "the system or code of morals of a particular person, religion, group, profession, etc." So even "ethics" has a foundation, and it is identified as "morals" from a particular source.

So what is "moral"? The dictionary defines it as "relating to, dealing with, or capable of making the distinction between, right and wrong in conduct." But that suggests that morals themselves are based on a code of right and wrong. And where can we find that code of "right and wrong"? For those in this country—if not now, then from our inception as a nation—that code of right and wrong comes from the Bible. It is our authority for right and wrong conduct or behavior—and it began with the Decalogue, also called the Ten Commandments.

So the Bible is our basis for knowing right and wrong, and therefore forms the basis of our moral outlook on all of life and, in turn, frames our view of ethical conduct in our living every aspect of our lives day to day. And if we are ethical in all our affairs with all men throughout our lives, we become known as honorable by reputation.

Therefore, to Be Honorable one must be ethical, moral, and adhere to the standards of the Holy Bible in all our conduct. Simple to understand, but not so simple to execute. But try we must—with His help.

How did Jesus Himself reflect this Behavior in all He did? There is no example or incident in all of the New Testament that reflects upon Him as anything but honorable. One of the more humorous examples of His being honorable and doing the right thing is when He and His disciple, Peter, were requested to pay their taxes (Matt. 17:24–27). He told Peter to go catch a fish and open its mouth, find their tax money, and go pay their tax. Don't you like Jesus's sense of humor?!

Be Involved

One of the surest ways for most adults to determine that a young man is starting to "get it" about growing up is to observe how he gets involved in the activities of home, school, church, and community. Some of you get into sports or extracurricular activities in school, and that is all good. Some of you go one better and start going after a job, not only to earn some money, but also to get some experience in the community. And that is good, too, as long as you keep your grades up. It prepares you for adulthood better by seeing that there is much to do and to be responsible for in life. It requires the juggling and balancing of many priorities and responsibilities while still doing well in all of them.

But then there are many young fellas who don't want to help around the house, much less in church. And yet those are two of the most reasonable and urgent places to get involved. Doing chores around the house should be almost second nature. I mean, how hard is it to look around and see what needs to be done and then do it without being asked? Let's face it, your mom and dad want and need you to begin as soon as possible to help them manage their home. You can do many things, like take care of your room, help with cleaning chores, help with cooking occasionally (it's a great thing to learn to cook while at home—it's not just for girls), do the yard, empty the trash, etc., etc. That is a BIG indicator that you are growing up to be responsible, by getting involved in what needs to be done.

That sort of involvement is what employers look for in an employee; are you a self-starter who observes and takes action to get things done well and quickly? It is the same as putting on the mind-set of the employer to see what needs to be done. That kind of proactive employee will quickly go far in any company.

Are you beginning to see how being involved in the wider life all around you is a sign that you are maturing? Well, there is still another area that needs you to become more involved as you mature. That is the church. If you are going to be a man for God, then you will necessarily become a churchman. Most young men wait way too long to be involved in this fascinating part of the Christian life. So what are some of the ways to become involved in this area?

There is, of course, the youth ministry. Here you will learn about the life in Christ and learn to live it. I write about that need in the chapter on Be Knowledgeable. Then there is the need to be involved in some of the many activities of the church. In fact, some of you, as you become juniors and seniors in high school and later on in your twenties, may actually want to join the men's ministry. When you begin to associate with the men of the church in Bible study, men's retreats, discipleship training, mentoring, church work days, mission outreach, etc., you accelerate your understanding of being a Man of Integrity and Godly Character. *If you associate with godly men as a young man, you become a better man* and *more quickly.* That is, of course, an excellent idea, because it prepares you to become an adult member of the church.

Some of you, as teenagers, may even decide that you want to further declare your maturity by sitting with your parents in the worship service, rather than always sitting with the youth group. Besides, you'll learn more of lasting value from adults or parents than from peers. It says that you want to go on toward your life as an adult, and that is just part of that "going on."

Remember the story about Jesus when He was twelve? His parents had come to Jerusalem for Temple worship, but when they left, Jesus, unknown to them, stayed on at the Temple. When they finally found Him, He was amazing all the teachers (rabbis) there with His wisdom and questions. So He knew He needed to be about His Father's business even at the young age of twelve. A quick sidenote: until the last two hundred years, children matured much earlier, for the most part. It had to do with the rigor of their education and the expectations that parents had for their children then. Frankly, young men of the church can help make that earlier maturing happen again in America.

Here is what the Bible says about this important business of becoming a godly man; it comes from Paul's extraordinary letter to the Romans in 12:9–13. "Let love be without hypocrisy. Abhor what is evil; cling to what is good. Be devoted to one another in brotherly love; give preference to one another in honor; not lagging behind in diligence, fervent in spirit, *serving the Lord*; rejoicing in hope, persevering in tribulation, devoted to prayer, *contributing to the needs of the saints*, practicing hospitality." This is the high calling to all men, young or old, in Christ Jesus.

So it is fundamental for you as a Christian young man to decide early on to grow in knowledge and grace about the things of God, and to reach out to become more involved in the work of the church. There are some excellent examples of this in most churches. Some of you may be teaching children's Sunday school quite competently. Some of you may have joined the orchestra or the sanctuary choir. Some of you may take responsible positions in the youth ministry. These are the kinds of things that you should aspire to do: to be of service at more and more levels within the church. Some of you may someday want to be a deacon or an elder; these are good things to want to be—to lead your church under God's direction, as determined through prayer. Let's face it, if you stretch yourself spiritually and intellectually, you learn and grow much faster. Your walk with God deepens and your value to Him in service increases markedly. It is the way to maturity in Christ. And if we truly want to become more like Him, then growth in ever-higher service is one way to do it, accompanied, of course, by diligent reading and study of His Word and prayer.

Jesus was involved in all manner of activities to establish His church on earth. And as a young man from His temple incident at age twelve to His baptism by John, the Bible says He "kept increasing in wisdom and stature, and in favor with God and man" (Luke 2:52). Now that's what you should aspire to do and be. So get involved as a churchman and grow in favor with God and man as a Man of Integrity and Godly Character.

Be Knowledgeable

The importance of this Behavior may be obvious to you, but we should spend a bit of time here to make sure you really know why it is important. First, as with all the others, let's get a dictionary definition of the word. It means "having or showing knowledge or intelligence."

So, it appears that it is not just important to have knowledge; you must also be able to use it, or display it as needed. And you should do that in your studies and in your work, and even in your play. Basically it's the same thing as having a tool for a certain job and knowing how to use it. Knowledge without application is close to worthless. In fact, if we don't know a lot about a lot of things, we are not too useful to ourselves or others. The more we know, the better able we are to negotiate this life in all its complexities.

Here are just some of the quotes from Proverbs about knowledge: "Wise men store up knowledge" (10:14) "Fools hate knowledge" (1:22); "The fear of the Lord is the beginning of knowledge" (1:7); "Through knowledge the righteous will be delivered" (11:9); "Every prudent man acts with knowledge, but a fool displays folly" (13:16); "A wise man is strong, and a man of knowledge increases power" (24:5). Then there is this quote from 2 Peter 3:18, "Grow in the grace and knowledge of our Lord and Savior Jesus Christ."

We have all heard someone say about another person, "He doesn't know what he's doing." We all place great store by someone knowing what they are doing. It is so important to us that we will not willingly follow someone whom we think doesn't know what he's doing. We silently demand that a leader know what he's doing. Therefore, one thing we can say for sure is that we humans do like to follow a leader who does appear to know what he is doing. Turning that around, then, if we aspire to be leaders in this life, we better learn all we can about as many things as we can, or we may not be able to lead. You will need to know a great deal about people to be a godly leader. And a godly leader grows from being a Man of Integrity and Godly Character. Leaders *know who they are, what they are doing, and why*—never forget that.

To learn a lot about a lot of things means you must have or develop a teachable spirit. You must be a person who enjoys learning—learning new things, reshaping old things once learned, with new information; constantly exploring the world of information to learn useful and substantial things about our world, our nation, your town, your school, your family, our God, His Word, your church, your friends, your neighbors, etc. So be teachable, and develop an appetite for learning more and more about more and more. On the other hand, be careful not to become one of those people who is always learning and never doing. The Bible says, "But prove yourselves doers of the word, and not merely hearers *who delude themselves*" (James 1:22).

One of the most damaging and pernicious (look it up if you don't know what it means) distractions from genuine learning in today's world is the electronic device. You must guard against allowing those things to suck you in and absorb your valuable time. To gain knowledge on any subject requires time and diligence on your part. Each of us has the same amount of time. To become knowledgeable men requires us to make the best choices on how we spend our limited and precious time. Can you think of activities that consume a lot of time but add nothing to your knowledge? Perhaps texting, Facebooking, TV, video games, etc.? Leisure is not a bad thing, but it must be done in balance with gaining useful knowledge to strengthen our spiritual, academic, and work life. The chronic overuse of some of the electronic devices can possibly trap you into an addiction that, in turn, could lead to a suspended adolescence emotionally and intellectually. You must take your stand against that if you are to become a knowledgeable, mature man.

Now is a good time to bring up a subject that for many in your generation is tough. I am talking about reading books. Many of you like the Internet, e-mail, Facebook, Twitter, etc. It has made you accustomed to small word bites, which are superficial in their content. Let me strongly encourage you to get back to reading books. You will deal with subjects in depth, and it will get you to thinking more deeply again. Obviously, one of the best books is the Bible. But there is a world of reading out there. At the end of this book I offer you suggestions for more reading on the topic of growing wise as a man.

Early in this discussion about being knowledgeable, I said that knowledge without application was close to worthless. And so it is. Could it not also be said that knowledge and/or ideas not well communicated are close to worthless? Of course. What am I getting at here? That's right, you need to learn to speak and write well—effectively! Writing well is greatly improved by reading *good* books and by writing essays to yourself on what you read. Speaking well is improved by taking every opportunity to speak in one of your groups like youth ministry, school, etc. Joining a drama group or debate team at school can help both your public speaking and your confidence under pressure (poise). Bottom line is that *all good leaders must be able to communicate lucidly and persuasively to be effective.*

What are some other things that you should know? Well, if you want to be a man for God, you better know a good deal about Him. You start with His Word, the Bible, and you read it with understanding. There are many good study aids available—and one of the best is a good study Bible in a literal translation, like *The MacArthur Study Bible: Revised & Updated Edition*. It came out recently (copyrighted in 2006) and has become the "gold standard" for many of us who have profited greatly from John MacArthur's Bible teaching over the years. And then, you should consider being part of a Bible study at your local church. Joining the men's ministry is a good idea, too.

You need to become thoroughly proficient in what it is you do, and there is no shortcut to that goal. You must make the pursuit of knowledge in that and allied fields a lifelong endeavor, because man's knowledge is always expanding. And you must have or develop an insatiable thirst for learning, which in turn requires that teachable spirit mentioned earlier. Sounds simple, and it is. But you must develop the resolve to make it happen. In fact, your going through this book is a foundational part of that whole process. I am encouraging you to keep on keeping on to the end of your life on earth. But the journey will be all the sweeter if you walk it through with God.

Was Jesus knowledgeable? Of course He was and is. After all, He spoke the entire universe into existence. But a more down-to-earth example of His knowledge was discussed in the previous chapter: He was twelve years old and was found by His parents in the Temple sitting among the teachers both listening to them and asking questions. All who heard Him were amazed at His understanding and answers. Could we not say that He had all knowledge of all things?

Be Merciful

You might be saying to yourself right now, "What does being merciful have to do with me becoming a Man of Integrity and Godly Character?" My answer: "Everything!" Anyone can pretend to be a better guy than everyone else. Anyone can, in other words, be a hypocrite, a JERK. A real man has a heart for other people, especially those in more difficult circumstances than his own. The dictionary says that "mercy" is "A refraining from harming or punishing offenders, enemies or other person's in one's power; kindness."

We have several excellent words that carry the meaning of "mercy" in them. One is compassion. If you have compassion for your fellow man, you will probably be merciful in your actions toward them. Another such word is "empathy." One who is empathetic about a situation is one who understands the situation even to the point of feeling the emotion, in most cases because that one has himself been in that situation. The founder of one overseas orphan ministry had the following phrase as his personal watchword: "Lord, let my heart be broken by those things that break Your heart." That's mercy writ large.

Here is something that may help you sort out the various words and thoughts about this area of thought.

> **Justice** means getting what we deserve.
>> **Mercy** means not getting what we deserve, but, ah,
>>> **Grace** means getting what we don't deserve.

Most of us associate Grace with what only God can do, but that is not so. If you read Philip Yancy's fine book, *What's So Amazing About Grace?* you will see that we, too, are to be dispensers of His Grace. Another short book you might consider reading on this very important subject of Grace is *The Grace and Truth Paradox* by Randy Alcorn. Remember, you must read books to grow in knowledge.

How about this?

> Bless those who persecute you; bless and do not curse. Rejoice with those who rejoice, and weep with those who weep. Be of the same mind toward one another; do not be haughty in mind, but associate with the lowly. Do not be wise in your own estimation. Never pay back evil for evil to anyone. Respect what is right in the sight of all men. If possible, so far as it depends on you, be at peace with all men. Never take your own revenge, beloved, but leave room for the wrath of God, for it is written, "Vengeance is Mine, I will repay," says the Lord. "But if your enemy is hungry, feed him, and if he is thirsty, give him a drink; for in so doing you will heap burning coals on his head."
> Do not be overcome by evil, but overcome evil with good. (Rom. 12:14–21)

And finally, but by no means least, is what God again says about all this mercy business. Look at Micah 6:8: "the Lord has told you what is good, and this is what He requires of you; to do what is right [just], to love **mercy**, and to walk humbly with your God" (NLT). Doesn't it just seem to say to you to be generous with all God gives you to all who need it, as though you were God's own heart, hands, and feet? It should.

And now about Jesus—was He merciful? There are many examples, but one of the most dramatic is when He calmed the wind and the hard rain about to sink their boat because He had mercy on His disciples. He healed hundreds of diseased people out of mercy (and a desire to show them the power of God). Then there is the ultimate act of mercy—to die on the cross to save us, who accept Him as Savior, from eternal death. Above all things, Jesus our Christ was most merciful. And we must follow Him in being merciful if we are ever to become like Him.

Be Prayerful

Being prayerful means "Given to frequent praying; devout."

What can a person pray about? Anything that is on your mind. Anything that distresses you or for which you want God's guidance. Anyone who needs God's help, healing, love, or salvation. Anytime you feel like praising and worshipping Him—it's all prayer. Prayer is no more complicated than having a conversation with God, and what an incredible privilege it is to be invited by the Almighty Creator of heaven and earth to speak with Him—about anything.

One of the great men of God, Martin Luther, a couple of centuries ago was asked how he managed to negotiate a busy day with such success and serenity. He said, "If I fail to spend two hours in prayer each morning, the devil gets the victory through the day. I have so much business I cannot get on without spending three hours daily in prayer."

But why do we pray? What is the fundamental reason we pray or should pray? Well, it goes back to why He created us—to have fellowship with Him. He wanted to love us and to have us want to love Him. He delights in our loving friendship. The Westminster (Shorter) catechism answers the question "What is the chief end of man?" with this answer: "Man's chief end is to Glorify God and enjoy Him forever." Without prayer, that would be impossible.

Maybe you've experienced this: when we spend frequent time with a friend, we each begin to take on some characteristics of the other. Have you noticed that some long-married couples seem to look alike or have similar mannerisms? In the very same way, as we spend more time conversing with our great God, over time we will begin to absorb and reflect His character and characteristics. We become more like Him. We will "look" like Him in our behavior—we will act like Him. And isn't that what a Christian's highest goal is—to become like Him?

And what should be the priority for prayer in our lives? The Book of the Acts of the Apostles has the definitive answer in verse forty-two of chapter two: "They were continually devoting themselves to the apostles' **teaching**, and to **fellowship**, to the **breaking of bread**, and to **PRAYER**." So there it is; prayer is one of the four basic activities of the church, any church. *Teaching* is the bedrock of any church, which helps us gain knowledge as we discussed in "Be Knowledgeable." *Fellowship* is one of the foundation blocks also—without it there is no partnership or sharing, which is vital to any organism. *Breaking of Bread* refers to the Lord's Supper or Communion—without it there is incomplete worship and reverence of God for whom He is and what He did to found the church. Finally, there is *prayer* as one of the founding four pillars of the church—*without it there is no spiritual growth and no real fellowship with our Almighty God.*

While pondering late at night how to articulate the importance of prayer to our spiritual life, I believe God gave me an analogy.

Picture in your mind a column of words under the title "BODY." Arrayed under that would be, for now, three words: FOOD, WATER, and BREATH. Now, envision another column headed by the title "SPIRIT." What word would you put opposite FOOD in this SPIRIT column? How about THE WORD or BREAD OF LIFE? What word would you put opposite WATER in this SPIRIT column? How about PRAISE, LIVING WATER, or WORSHIP? And, finally, what word would you put in the SPIRIT column opposite BREATH? How about PRAYER? What's the point?

Our bodies can live for weeks without food, for days without water, but only minutes without breath. And, if you are a Christian, so it is with our spiritual selves: you can survive spiritually without reading the Word for a while, but you won't thrive. Without worshipping and praising God with the outflowing of Living Water, most of us will get by again, but only for a while; our souls yearn to worship God, and if we don't we begin to shrivel spiritually. But without prayer and confession, without communing with God regularly, you will quite literally begin to die spiritually. A Christian who lives without prayer will walk about with little or no evidence of the Holy Spirit of God in him. Without breath, our bodies become quickly brain dead, and then the body dies. Without prayer, our spirit loses touch with the Holy Spirit of God and we become "heart" dead, followed by hypocrisy in our behavior. Prayer keeps us real and vibrant for God's use in the lives of others. And we depend on wisdom from God's Spirit, which we gain from spending time with Him in prayer and in His Word.

> *"You may as soon find a living man that does not breathe, as a living Christian that does not pray."*
>
> —Matthew Henry

To ensure you do not miss the important discipline of commitment ("Be Disciplined") that is part of being prayerful, I repeat it here.

How does one commit to God? Just tell God every day, from the bottom of your heart, that you want Him to lead you every step of the way that day. Some people get up a bit earlier every day to spend time with the Lord with prayer, Bible reading, and quiet time to just sit before Him and praise Him for Who He is. You can read a few Bible verses, and/or you can pray to Him about issues in your life where you need His help. One excellent online site for a daily Bible verse and lesson is from Moody Bible Institute; it is www.todayintheword.com. *You will grow in spiritual strength if you practice such a "Quiet Time" each day.* It doesn't have to be a long time, maybe five or ten minutes at first. He will guide you into a deeper time with Him as He thinks you're ready. Just enjoy Him and worship Him—for He is surely worth it, wouldn't you say?! After a while you will find that you miss the strength and comfort that such a time gives you when you miss a day or two.

As an assist for you, I recommend you get a copy of Robert Boyd Munger's booklet entitled *My Heart—Christ's Home*.[4] It is the best dollar you may ever spend. It will help you understand from Christ's perspective how important "quiet time" is to Him for your ultimate good.

So, by all means possible "seek His face" each day of your life. Pray for others often. Purpose to find a like-minded young man with whom you can partner in prayer. To be

---

[4] Robert Boyd Munger, *My Heart—Christ's Home* (Downer's Grove, IL: InterVarsity Press, 1986).

someone's partner in prayer means that you care enough about him to call him up or go see him to ask him for prayer about an issue you have—or alternatively to ask him if you can join him in praying for something in his life that needs prayer. This is a wise thing to do in this life of confusion, doubt, evil, and compromise; find someone with whom you can covenant to be in frequent prayer. It keeps us accountable to someone who really cares about us staying pure and straight.

I cannot recommend more highly to you any activity that will reward you more handsomely than to pray daily with the God Who made you. John Wesley, a famous evangelist who spent two hours in prayer daily, said two thought-provoking things about prayer: (1) prayer is where the action is, and (2) God does nothing except in response to believing prayer. Another old evangelist, Sidlow Baxter, said, "Men may spurn our appeals, reject our message, oppose our arguments, despise our persons, but they are helpless against our prayers." *Prayer coupled with the reading of the Bible cannot help but turn any of us into Men of Integrity and Godly Character.*

Christ Jesus Himself spent about a third of His time in prayer, day or night. He did nothing on His own; He did only what God His Father told Him to do. And Jesus received His instructions the way all of us should—through prayer. Not a bad model for us. So pray. God is listening and wants to help us along life's way. He promised.

Be Respectful

The dictionary says that being respectful is "to show deference or due regard; to show honor or esteem for." It is widely known that the culture of Southern states requires boys and girls to grow up saying "Yes, ma'am" and "No, ma'am," and "Thank you, sir" and "Yes, please, sir." Children are taught, or once were taught, to be respectful in their language to their elders. That excellent Behavior is looked upon with derision in some parts of the country, because the children in those cultures are not taught to respect their elders, or anyone else, for that matter. It has led to a growing incivility of the nation's culture.

One of the ugly results of this is increasing use of vulgar, coarse, and profane language in the public square, movies, and on the air (radio and TV). There are words commonly used today as acceptable that are, in fact, crude and coarse. Some of them are pissed off, butt, ass, screwed (in many forms), snot, crap, BS, etc. Learn to curb your tongue from gutter-slang when in conversation. Then, of course, there are the really foul words—the so-called four-letter words—that are profane, obscene, vulgar, and/or repugnant, and should never be used. Some have said that to use such words is to reveal that you have a limited vocabulary; I would say that it reveals a lame brain—a disrespectful attitude toward others.

There is nothing wrong and everything right with being considerate of others, no matter their age. How hard is it for any of us to say "Thank you" to someone who has done something nice for us? Or even to write a thank-you note to someone who has had you to his or her home for a meal, or given you a gift? To do otherwise displays an arrogance toward others that is not warranted. Think about it.

The idea of being considerate, or respectful, suggests the idea of humility, wouldn't you say? Let's look at what scripture has to say about this. Romans 12:3, "For through the grace given to me I say to every one among you not to think more highly of himself than he ought to think; but to think so as to have sound judgment, as God has allotted to each a measure of faith." One thing for sure you ought to take away from this thought-provoking quote is that *if you aren't all puffed up about yourself, you can think more clearly, more soundly.* And that's true, isn't it? If we get all caught up in how great we think we are, we just aren't thinking straight and cannot make good decisions. It is a hollow conceit that one person thinks he is better than someone else. We may each have different talents and abilities, and we do—but that is no reason to think better of yourself than someone else, even if you are better in something than someone else.

Being respectful also carries the obligation of being obedient. Another way to say it is disobedience shows our disrespect toward another person. So we should always strive to be not just borderline obedient, but to do more than is expected of us. Scripture points out that when someone asks you to walk a mile with them, walk two. That was a reference to when a Roman soldier told a Hebrew man to carry his pack and equipment a mile or so, the Christian Hebrew was expected by Christ to go that and more for the soldier, as though he enjoyed serving him. And that story shows another side of being obedient—being helpful—on purpose. Show respect to others and then do not be surprised if they show you respect; that's just the way it works in life.

Another aspect of Be Respectful that may not have crossed your mind is the serious and courteous act of being on time, even early, to a meeting or an appointment. Think about it: if you have taken the care to be on time for an appointment, and then others arrive late so that the meeting or business at hand is unable to start on time, what do you think those who are late are "saying" to those who were on time? Frankly, they are "saying" that you are unimportant to them, that they do not respect you, that they are the only ones who count, that the world revolves around them . . . So be on time to all your appointments; it shows that you respect others' time as much as you value your own time. And remember, being "on time" literally means arriving early enough (ten to fifteen minutes) so the meeting can begin at the appointed time.

Here are a few more things you can do that show that you have respect for others:

- If seated, rise when a woman or older person enters the room.
- When shaking hands, give a firm grip and look the person straight in the eye.
- When on public transportation, offer your seat to a woman or an elderly man as a sign of respect.
- When our national anthem is played, you should stand at attention and render honor to

our flag by placing your right hand over your heart.

One last area that few think about in the area of being respectful is in your manner of dress, your clothing. To wear slovenly clothing (torn, ripped, faded, dirty, showing underwear, etc.) or inappropriate clothing (shorts and flip-flops to a nice affair [symphonic concert, church, funeral, sit-down dinner at a home, business meeting, hospital visitation, etc.]) is another of those behaviors that displays your contempt for others. Now I realize the US culture has begun to "condone" many forms of dress that would have been considered insulting only twenty years ago, but that does not mean that you should bow to those lower "standards," like wearing your cap inside, or worse, at the table. Just as some began leading the way to lower standards of dress and the usually less desirable comportment (look it up) that accompanies it, so you can begin to lead the way forward to a better cultural standard of dress and comportment. Most of what is in this book is about that very thing, helping you see the better, even best, way to behave—so that you can be a *leader* in all these Behaviors.

Can you think of any other area of your life, say at home, where you should probably Be Respectful? You got it. You must respect your parents. The Bible says it this way in Exodus 20:12, which lays out the fifth commandment of the ten: "Honor your father and your mother, that your days may be prolonged in the land which the Lord your God gives you." That is the first commandment with a promise—and it seems to suggest it could cut both ways. So always honor your parents.

Jesus was respectful of all, whether Roman, Jew, or Gentile. About the only time He spoke disrespectfully was to the Pharisees when He called them "whitewashed tombs" (Matt. 23:27). Even then it was for a beneficial purpose—to attempt to turn them from their legalistic, hypocritical ways that were leading the Jewish people astray.

Be Responsible

The dictionary says that being responsible means you "readily assume obligations, duties, etc.; you're dependable; reliable; you're able to distinguish between right and wrong and to think and act rationally—and hence accountable for one's behavior." Do you have a friend whom you consider responsible? Are you a responsible person?

Do you begin to see a connection here with some of the other Behaviors we have talked about? "Right and wrong" were covered in the section on Be Honorable, and being accountable for one's behavior echoes some things discussed in "Be Disciplined." So these Behaviors should now be tying themselves together in your mind into a coherent and cohesive whole, wouldn't you say? And that is exactly where we are trying to take all this. We want it to stick in your mind and heart as Behaviors that make sense, hang together, and make you want to be this kind of man. What kind of man? A Man of Integrity and Godly Character. That's a young man who wants to stop being a Sheep to learn how to be a Shepherd—a leader.

One of the surest things you must do to Be Responsible is to **own** your roles in life as a trustworthy student, a son, a friend, a worker, a teacher, a leader, and later on—a husband, a father, etc. (I talk about these future roles a bit in the last chapter, entitled "Looking Ahead.") By owning your roles in life, you will stand out from the many who only want to do enough to get by (if that much). That's no way to lead a life. There is simply no satisfaction in being a taker (instead of giver), a quitter (instead of winner), or a goof-off (instead of being a man with a *fire in his belly* to accomplish something worthwhile with his life). Which one are you? Sadly today, too many young men are content just to grow older, but not grow up.

The great satisfactions in life center around the concept of working hard and achieving tough goals and objectives. You might just be surprised at how many men and women in life don't even want to do the bare minimum; they want the government to take care of them without working. Taking from the government (or anyone) when you are very well able to work was once viewed by Americans as a humiliating disgrace. Even those who were not able to work back then were still ashamed to take a handout. It was ingrained in all of us to work for what we got, and for many it still is. Able-bodied people who won't work are the parasites of our society; they live off the hard work of others (through the redistribution of tax money from America's workers to the scammers, the welfare queens, and others who can work but won't).

Following along in exactly that vein, this comes from the Bible: **"if anyone is not willing to work, then he is not to eat, either"** (2 Thess. 3:10b). There are other passages in the book of Proverbs that show that the person who is diligent in his work will be rewarded by God Himself. Proverbs 22:29 says, "Do you see a man skilled in his work? He will stand before kings; he will not stand before obscure men." Take a look at Proverbs 21:25; 24:12d, and 29, too.

One of the most important parts of being responsible is to be dependable. Because lack of dependability is so prevalent in our society, you will stand out head and shoulders above other employees if your boss can always depend on you to be where you are supposed to be, when you're supposed to be, and do what you're supposed to do. Dependability marks you as a man headed for higher responsibilities in your company. If you are not dependable, you also are not responsible. The two go hand in hand.

Never whine. Whining is infantile. It is immature. It shows you to be a small-minded person who is always thinking about yourself and what's in it for you. If you are being treated unfairly, change your attitude and/or change your job—but don't whine. There is an old expression that says, "When things get tough, the tough get going." Notice it did not say "the tough get to whining."

Another aspect of being responsible is that you determine to be truthful. Never lie! It's part of the Decalogue, one of the Ten Commandments, not the Ten Suggestions. There are a few examples of lying in the Bible where lying appears to be condoned because the purpose of the lie was to save lives. Examples are Rahab hiding the Hebrew spies at Jericho, midwives lying about why they did not kill Hebrew babies in Egypt, etc.

Other than that exceptional case (lying to save lives), make your mind up right now that you will not lie ever, not even one of those little "white lies." There is no such thing as a "little white lie"—even that fiction is a lie from the devil himself; and the Bible calls the devil the "Father of Lies." If you have lied in the past, then go to God and ask for His forgiveness (He is always ready to forgive you).

Finally, to Be Responsible you must learn to manage His money and your affairs biblically. You must consider yourself as always working for God. After all, He created you and He sustains you by providing you labor for which you receive money, which in turn buys food, clothing, shelter, transportation, entertainment, etc. This would be a good time for you (and your dad or mentor) to read the Parable of the Talents in Matthew 25:14–30; it illustrates the tragedy of wasted opportunity. He expects us all to manage all that comes in to our hands with intelligence and wisdom. There is much more in scripture, especially in the Proverbs, about managing your affairs and the money He gives you. Read it to grow wise. Then do it to become responsible.

There is no question about Jesus being responsible. From His youth to the cross, He steadfastly followed the plan given Him by God, His Father. In my view, there has never been a more responsible man born. He knew He was responsible to His Father to provide the only way of salvation for every human being. Wow!

One of the most important components of being a Man of Integrity and Godly Character is to Be Responsible.

Be Tough Minded

The dictionary defines "tough" as "Strong of physique; robust; hardy; displaying mental or moral firmness; practical and realistic rather than emotional or sentimental." That is the state of mind that we are to adopt if we are to not only survive the trials and troubles of this life, but also to thrive in spite of them.

A man must be strong not just in his body, but also in his mind. He must be emotionally strong so that he can be morally and spiritually strong. You must be tough enough to make the right decisions—even though you might like to do some of the wrong things because it looks like fun. Some tests in life do not give you a second chance, like some drugs. Do you know anyone who woke up one day and said, "I want to be a drug addict when I grow up?" Of course not. Yet some drugs are so dangerously addictive that one experiment with it can addict you and ruin you for life. Just do not do things that may look "cool" but are just a dead end (pun intended).

A person can be so tough minded, however, that he is unbending and unyielding when being resilient or flexible would serve better. We all need to develop the wisdom to know when to stand firm or bend without breaking, to roll with the punches of life and still come back strong.

One of the greatest aspects of being tough minded is to be comfortable in your own skin. Someone who is comfortable in his own skin, an old expression that says a lot, is someone who has made up his mind about who he is and what he believes, and knows where he is going. Someone like that cannot be distracted by all the temptations in life, the sex, the booze, the drugs, the illegal activities, the constant over-the-top entertainment offerings on the media, even the hedonistic (look it up) social gatherings, etc.

Tough-minded men are solid men who have thought it all through with the help of able coaches, parents, older friends, etc. They are young men who have sought out such good counsel and have followed the solid advice and applied it to their lives. Such men are secure in who they are and they don't need the "crowd" to tell them what to do and be. They are their own man—a Man of Integrity and Godly Character—the kind of man that other men seek out for counsel and advice and leadership. They are Sheep who have become Shepherds.

A danger of being a counselor to others is that you may become "puffed up" or full of pride. To remain humble requires that you be tough minded enough to remember who you are—an imperfect person being used of God to help others. Your wisdom, strength, and humility are what draw men to you. Lose any one of them, and you've lost what is of value to others. Be humble. Proverbs 22:4 says, "The reward of humility and the fear [awestruck reverence] of the Lord are riches, honor, and long life."

The last thing I want to say about being tough minded is to always mean what you say. And a close corollary to that is to never make excuses. All men must be able to trust you implicitly, and that means more than just not lying. They must know that what you say is what they can depend upon. In other words, you speak the truth, no matter the circumstances or the person. *If your word is not reliable, then you are not reliable.* No one will care to do business with you. So, make up your mind now to be tough minded . . . for all of your life.

Jesus had to Be Tough Minded to endure all the insults and abuse, and ultimately His death on the cross, for us. In short, Jesus evidences every one of these twelve Behaviors abundantly—and is therefore the single best role model for each of our lives. Think about it! Though we can't be better than our ultimate model, let us all strive to be like Him! And that, young sir, will be your lifelong quest.

Looking Ahead

I want to cover five conditions or situations that you may face as you move into the future from high school. They are Work, Higher Education, Marriage, Fatherhood, and Operating in the World. I want to share a few observations about these in brief "pictures." There is much repetition here, so you need read only the area that interests you at that moment.

Work

If you are going to forego a college or university education and go straight into the workforce, allow me a word or two of counsel.

1. If you must live at home until you are established, then get established in record time and get out truly on your own as soon as possible. Do not become a ward of your parents. Offer to pay your way for food, roof, and utility share. Their job of rearing you to be a Man of Integrity and Godly Character is finished, so you must begin now to "pay your own way." And if you don't "get it" that you are now to support yourself and instead want to hang around the house without a job, occupying space and giving off CO_2, do not be surprised when your parents or guardian literally kick you out of their house. They

will do you no favor by allowing you to become a human "weed."

2. Join a church and be stubbornly faithful to attend, even to join. Then become active. You are not saved to sit and soak, but to stand, to serve, and to share the Gospel.

3. Do not—let me say this again—DO NOT get romantically involved until you are out on your own. Hormones being what they are, you will want to at least date, so do it smartly. Do not date a woman who is not also a Christian; that admonition in scripture about being unequally yoked (2 Cor. 6:14) was not "just" a suggestion. Speaking of hormones, in the "world" it is *okay* to have sexual relations anytime consenting adults feel like it. According to God, Who invented sex, that is wrong; sexual relations, in His judgment (the only one that counts), have only one acceptable context—marriage.

4. You have no business getting married until you can support her fully on your own. Even then, you should not do so until you have a nest egg (about six months net pay) put away in savings for the ALWAYS-rainy day that is right around the corner. You must never marry if either of you has any debt, unless it is a mortgage that you can easily handle without tapping your nest egg. In addition, you must have a solid job in which you are a valued and respected performer with recognized advancement prospects into the future. Also, your vehicle must be paid off (remember? No debt!). Why so strict here?

Because a wife and babies cost money—lots of money.
5. Violate this advice and you risk jeopardizing your future for an uncomfortably long chunk of your life. How do I know this? I spent over ten years counseling singles and couples from a five-state area around Virginia on how to manage their finances biblically. This advice I just gave you, if followed, will assure that you do not become like one of the hundreds of people who came to me to help them get their lives out of the financial trash can.

Higher Education

If you are going to go to a university with the intent of entering a profession—or to a vocational or technical college with the intent of entering a technical field—allow me a few helpful observations.

1. If you must live at home while attending vo-tech or a university (and living at home is a good idea, if your parents can stand it), then do all in your diligent power to **not** take out any (no, not one) student loans. That means a job, a good part-time job. Offer to pay your way for food, roof, and utility share while living at home—though your parents may insist that they do this as part of their contribution to your higher education. If your parents want to pay for part of your education, that is wonderful, of course. But let's get something very clear here—it is your responsibility and yours alone to get that higher education. Their responsibility to God is to raise you to adulthood. So when you reach eighteen in our culture, their job of

rearing you to be a Man of Integrity and Godly Character is finished.

2. Join a church and be stubbornly faithful to attend, even to join. Because of your studies and your part-time job(s), you may not be able to become active. But after graduation, if you stay in the same area, do become active. A Christian man is not saved to sit and soak, but to stand, to serve and to share the Gospel. And no matter where you go in the world with your work, do not shortchange yourself with God; always join a local church and get involved.

3. Do not—let me say this again—DO NOT get romantically involved until you are out on your own and well established in your profession. Hormones being what they are, you will want to at least date, so do it smartly. Do not date a woman who is not also a Christian; that admonition in Scripture about being unequally yoked (2 Cor. 6:14) was not "just" a suggestion. Speaking of hormones, in the "world" it is *okay* to have sexual relations anytime consenting adults feel like it. According to God, Who invented sex, that is wrong; sexual relations in His judgment (the only one that counts) have only one acceptable context—marriage.

4. You have no business getting married until you can support her fully on your own. Even then, you should not do so until you have a nest egg (about six months net pay) put away in savings for the ALWAYS-rainy day that is right around the corner. You must never marry if either of you has any debt, unless it is a mortgage that you can easily handle without tapping your nest

egg. In addition, you must have a solid job in which you are a valued and respected performer with recognized advancement prospects into the future. Also, your vehicle must be paid off (remember? No debt!). Why so strict here? Because a wife and babies cost money—lots of money.

5. Violate this advice and you risk jeopardizing your future for an uncomfortably long chunk of your life. How do I know this? I spent over ten years counseling singles and couples from a five-state area around Virginia on how to manage their finances biblically. This advice I just gave you, if followed, will assure that you do not become like one of the hundreds of people who came to me to help them get their lives out of the financial trash can.

Marriage

Some of the counsel I have for you in this joyfully important area of our lives comes from very painful lessons in my life. So I do not offer counsel lightly or frivolously. Marriage is the second relationship that God orchestrated. The first was His creation of man, then woman, to be in lifelong love relationships with Him. His most ardent desire for us on earth is for each of us to form a lifelong love relationship with a member of the opposite gender. If done correctly, according to His rules, we can experience the transcendent joy in our lives together that He knows we can and should have. Here's a book that may help: Gary Chapman, *Covenant Marriage*.

1. I have observed that the marriages that seem to thrive well are those that came into being after the man had established himself well in his field of

endeavor. "Why is that?" I asked myself. My many years of counseling couples in how to manage their affairs biblically suggests that those who marry after the man is well established in his field have far fewer money problems. Ten percent of all marriages break up within the first five years. Another twenty-five percent break up before the ten-year anniversary. Ninety percent of those divorcing said that the reason was money problems. By the way, those statistics are the same for Christian and non-Christian couples—a sad commentary on Christians NOT listening to God's advice. So do not marry until you are (a) out of all debt—unless you have a "comfortable" mortgage, (b) have significant savings and/or investments, and (c) are, as stated at the outset, *firmly* successful in your chosen field of endeavor.

2. This next point should have been first, perhaps, because it is an absolute in my book. Do not ever marry a woman who is not also a Christian; do not become unequally yoked (2 Cor. 6:14). I'll go one step further and say she, as a Christian, should have about the same level of zeal and commitment to the Lord as you do. Red hot and lukewarm do not mix well—and can become a source of confusion, if not outright contention. Why do I feel so strongly about this very serious admonition in scripture? Because when I came to Christ after seventeen years of marriage, I went "all out" for God; my wife never did. We became unequally yoked. The marriage eventually, for that and other reasons, came unwound some twenty-plus years later. Seldom, if ever, are there winners in divorce, though there are times when divorce is appropriate to save a life or escape infidelity. If you like pain, and feel like you are

the exception to God's rule about being unequally yoked, then go ahead and throw your life away. Remember— I warned you.

3. Be sure you both are on the same page when it comes to the *stuff* of life. Stuff like budgeting and financial management. Stuff like your goals in life, short term and long term. Stuff like how many children you want to have. Stuff like will the wife, then mother, stay home to raise the children and for how long? Stuff like *agreeing* with God that the man is to be the leader in the home and on how you two will discipline your children (even more important if you have a blended family later on). And how about homeschooling? Stuff like pets, if any (this is a big one, because some folks have become irrational about their pets and animal rights, so you must sort this one out early on). Stuff like ministry ideas. Stuff like will relatives live with you or not, and if so, under what conditions. Stuff like nutrition and food fads, and who cooks, etc. Stuff like "Don't sweat the small stuff; it's all small stuff anyway" (this one is about who wants to be the obsessive-compulsive, controlling person who insists on things being their way—like where the toothpaste tube is pushed [no kidding], etc., etc.; it's poison, don't go there). Get all these things out into the open before you get married.

4. Most importantly, you must each realize that marriage must be a 100/100 proposition. A 50/50 deal is a recipe for disaster sooner than later. Love of God requires your ALL in mind, body, soul, strength, and spirit; the same applies in the mortal realm between spouses. Marriage is not to be a *competitive contest*;

it is to be a *coordinated collaboration* for your joy and God's Glory. After all, the word collaboration means to "labor together," to co-labor in the vineyard of marriage. Think of a triangle with Christ at the peak and you and your wife at the lower corners. As you each grow in your relationships with Christ, you cannot help but grow closer to each other as you ascend the legs of the triangle in knowledge, love, and obedience. So give your all to Him and to her, and experience the true joy of the Lord in your marriage. To God alone be the Glory!

Fatherhood

If you two decide to have children, you must first back up and decide a few other things before going ahead with this momentous decision that can, with the right attention from you and your wife, be one of the great joys of your life. But I will tell you frankly that if you do not give your children the time and attention they need, the entire enterprise can be a disaster and one of the biggest heartaches of your life. *In fact, this is the issue that animates my passion for helping young men become Men of Integrity and Godly Character.* **Dads MUST spend time with their sons to teach them by action and word what they must know to become such a man.** *It takes time and deliberate attention.*

1. So now let's get one very basic thing settled right from the get-go. Your job as a parent is not to be a "buddy" to your children; *your job (from God) is to raise adults, not kids.* Basically, you are to raise your man-child to become a Man of Integrity and Godly Character, just like we have talked about for the major part of this book. You can't do that wisely or well if you insist on being a buddy-buddy, "let's be

pals" kind of dad. Nor can you do it by belittling or demeaning your son for poor behavior. Attacking your children with angry or insulting words leaves deep scars on their self-worth, which may never heal (I know this firsthand). Your job is to encourage right behavior and discourage wrong behavior, by wise discipline, without crushing their spirit. The Bible makes it abundantly clear that corporal punishment be administered wisely and prudently, as required.

2. You must decide to be the man in the house and the spiritual leader that God calls all husbands/fathers to be. You need to lead your family in daily devotion and in prayer. When you are traveling, you must ask your wife to conduct the daily devotion and prayer. You must establish that your family reverences and worships Almighty God as its foundational activity. You must all be active in a local, Christ-centered, Bible-believing church. That is the example your son needs to follow if he is to indeed become a Man of Integrity and Godly Character. One of the most memorable sights your young children will ever experience is to "catch" you on your knees in your prayer place. He must emulate you, Dad. *If you aren't up to the challenge, then don't bring any children, male or female, into this world.* Your solemn responsibility is to God and God alone in this challenging undertaking of raising children, er, adults. We get only one pass at this serious business of raising our progeny to be Adults of Integrity and Godly Character; there are no do-overs.

3. Let's look at what the Bible has to say about the Christian home and children. Go to Colossians 3:18–

21, "Wives be subject to your husbands, as is fitting in the Lord. Husbands, love your wives and do not be embittered against them. Children, be obedient to your parents in all things, for this is well-pleasing to the Lord. Fathers, do not exasperate your children, so that they will not lose heart." Note here that though God has given you authority over your children, you are NOT to abuse that authority; you are in every sense accountable to God for the rearing of the children he may give you. It is a high calling to be taken seriously.

4. One additional Scripture would be helpful here, too. It is the classic from Ephesians 6:1–4. "Children, obey your parents in the Lord, for this is right. Honor your Father and Mother [which is the first commandment with a promise], so that it may be well with you, and that you may live long on the earth. Fathers, do not provoke your children to anger, but bring them up in the discipline and instruction of the Lord." It strikes me that you can't do this disciplining and instructing unless you are spending TIME with your children. Nor can you do it if you are a bully; no one listens to or likes, much less loves, a bully. You see, don't you, this serious business of rearing godly adults cannot be done casually; it is deliberate, takes great patience, and it is time consuming. See Deuteronomy 6:4–9.

5. There are many fine books available to help you do your job, Dad. In addition, there is a fine movie about all this from the Sherwood Baptist Church in Albany, Georgia; it is entitled *Courageous*. This bunch put out other blockbuster Christian movies-with-a-message like *Flywheel*, *Facing the Giants*, and *Fireproof*. I

recommend you consider putting all four of them in your home movie library. You can view them with your sons (and daughters) and discuss what you all are seeing and thinking about. Good support study materials for each movie are available from the LifeWay bookstores.

6. At this point in your life, you must reassess your priorities. They should line up something like this: God, Wife, Children, Work, Church, Recreation, etc. Here's a book, in addition to those in the Suggested Reading at the end, that may help you with this exciting but demanding phase of your life: Steve Farrar, *Anchorman*.

Operating in the World

"Do not love the world nor the things in the world. If anyone loves the world, the love of the Father is not in him. For all that is in the world, the lust of the flesh and the lust of the eyes and the boastful pride of life, is not from the Father, but is from the world. And the world is passing away, and also its lusts; but the one who does the will of God lives forever" (1 John 2:15–17).

We Christians, among all creatures, are most peculiar. We are *in* the world, but we are no longer *of* the world. We are passing through; this is not our home. Yet we are here, and we are to make the best of it. We are to be salt and light; what does that look like?

The principal activity that we are to do all of our lives is to help others find the one true God by sharing, with all who will listen, the Good News of salvation from Hell and for Heaven that is obtained solely through Jesus Christ by God's

Grace through the faith that He, again, gives us (John 14:6, Eph. 2:8–9).

It strikes me that had more strong Christians been involved and engaged in the affairs of our nation at all levels since 1945 (end of World War II), we would not be in the immoral jam we're in now. A book out in 2011 by Jonathon Cahn (*The Harbinger*[5]) has the following stunningly accurate information:

> In the middle of the twentieth century America began officially removing God from its national life. It abolished prayer and Scripture in the public schools. As ancient Israel had removed the Ten Commandments from its national consciousness, so America did likewise, removing the Ten Commandments from public view, banning it from its public squares, and taking it down, by government decree, from its walls. As it was in ancient Israel, so too in America, God was progressively driven out of the nation's public life. The very mention of *God* or *Jesus* in any relevant context became more and more taboo and unwelcome unless for the purpose of mockery and attack. That which had once been revered as sacred was now increasingly treated as profanity. And as God was driven out, idols were brought in to replace Him.

And what are "idols"? According to Cahn, they are:

> [I]dols of sensuality, idols of greed, of money, success, comfort, materialism, pleasure, sexual immorality, self-worship, self-obsession. The sacred increasingly

---

[5] Jonathon Cahn, *The Harbinger* (Florida: Charisma House Book Group, 2011), 20–21.

disappeared, and the profane took its place. It was another kind of spiritual amnesia; the nation forgot its foundations,* its purpose, and its calling. The standards and values it had long upheld were now abandoned. What it had once known as immoral, it now accepted. Its culture was increasingly corrupted by the corrosion of sexual immorality, growing continuously more crude and vulgar. A wave of pornography began penetrating its media. The same nation that had once been dedicated to spreading God's light to the nations now filled the world with the pornographic and obscene.

You may recall my discussing this very issue in the last half of our preface.

So now it becomes clear that another activity we Christians are to engage in all our lives is to get involved in the affairs of mankind. Do not be put off by those who would ignorantly say that Christians are not to be involved in the affairs of the world, because we are to triumph in our involvement in those affairs. Whatever you do, do it all to the Glory of God.

Run for public office. Politics today seems to be a very ugly business; campaigning is brutal and vicious. So, how can that change? When good and godly men and women get involved in the process and when enough of such men and women get into office to begin to turn the ugliness around, politics might begin to resemble a worthy occupation for worthy people. Is that pie in the sky? Nope, it just will take the best of all the Behaviors I have written about here in every candidate to begin to slowly turn the great ship of state back to a true and righteous course. Will you need God's help? Yes, every step of the way to it and through it.

So, I am encouraging those few of you who will see this great challenge and will want to become part of bringing America back to her original course as is so brilliantly laid out in our God-given Constitution. Run for office and do your great God proud! You do know, don't you, that this nation was discovered, founded, developed, and prospered by God Himself to be His great Christian experiment in government? It was and can be again! The secret is to bring America back to God, and none of us can do that without Him.

Now, do not stop here, please. I urge you to complete your work by reading carefully the epilogue.

Epilogue

Let me address something that has so far gone unstated. It is time to make it abundantly clear—the Holy Bible—the Word of God is the Truth of God for the People of God. I have unapologetically and frequently quoted the Bible because of His Truth about the topic under discussion. In effect, I have used His Word to "prove" the accuracy of my words.

His Word is infallible, devoid of error, and worthy of unending study, for it is God's revealed Truth on planet earth. Several hundred Old Testament prophecies about Christ's first coming made hundreds of years before He came were all fulfilled precisely as prophesied. There is no doubt, then, that the many prophecies about His Second Coming made in both the Old and New Testaments also will be precisely fulfilled exactly as promised. It is God's book. It is absolutely trustworthy because He is the author; it is His story. The Bible says this about itself:

> All scripture is inspired by God and profitable for teaching, for reproof, for correction, for training in righteousness; that the man of God may be adequate, equipped for every good work (2 Tim. 3:16–17).

There are a number of miscellaneous thoughts that I shall record here for you to ponder to further your maturing into a man worth following and emulating. These words are for you and also for you to teach your sons when the time comes. Remember that the third[6] most important responsibility you have in this life is to raise up godly adults, and especially to raise up strong, godly men (some may even be your own children).

Behavior, good or bad, always has consequences, good or bad . . .

Never let yourself be trapped into serving money and the world system. As a child of the King, your goal is souls for Him. Mere money pales next to that lofty objective. Love God, not money. "For the love of money is a root of all sorts of evil, and some by longing for it have wandered away from the faith and pierced themselves with many griefs" (1Tim. 6:10).

"A good name is more desired than great wealth;
Favor is better than silver and gold."
—Proverbs 22:1

"Train up a child in the way he should go, Even when he is old he will not depart from it."
—Proverbs 22:6

There is only one right way—God's Way, the Way of Life. That way is specified in great detail in the Book of Proverbs. Early training in righteousness should secure lifelong habits, and

---

[6] The single most important responsibility for you in this life is to serve God and His Kingdom after giving your life to Jesus Christ. Joshua (24:15) said, "If it is disagreeable in your sight to serve the Lord, choose for yourselves today whom you will serve; as for me and my house, we will serve the Lord." The second most important responsibility you have in this life, if God leads you to marry, is to love your wife as Christ also loved the church and gave Himself up for her (Eph. 5:25). Of paramount importance, when selecting a church to serve, find one that is solidly Christ centered and teaches and preaches the Bible only! Nothing less will do; hear me, please!

when you're a parent you must require it. Nonetheless, even with right training in the Way, the devil and the world all too often will corrupt the early righteous training. So be diligent and faithful to always teach the right Way, that your conscience before God is clear.

For you dads reading this, I'd like to suggest you think about giving your son a special ceremony making his becoming a man in your eyes, say, on their fifteenth or sixteenth birthday. There is an excellent book about this idea in *Rite of Passage: A Father's Blessing* by Jim McBride. Jim says, "Why does anyone need a book on a rite of passage? Because inviting a teenager into adulthood on purpose is better than letting it happen by accident. I believe it is part of our God-given responsibility in the stewardship of the lives of our children to call out the man in our boys and the woman in our girls."[7] It's an inspiring read.

> "But seek first His kingdom and His righteousness, and all these things will be added to you."
> —Matthew 6:33

> "Not everyone who calls out to me, 'Lord, Lord' will enter the Kingdom of Heaven, but he who does the will of My Father who is in heaven will enter."
> —Matthew 7:21

> "It is the blessing of the Lord that makes rich, and He adds no sorrow to it."
> —Proverbs 10:22

---

[7] McBride, Jim. *Rite of Passage: A Father's Blessing* (Chicago: Moody Publishers, 2011).

"Trust in the Lord with all your heart and do not lean on your own understanding. In all your ways acknowledge Him, and He will make your paths straight."
—Proverbs 3:5–6 (the author's Life Verse*)

"Be anxious for nothing, but in everything by prayer and supplication with thanksgiving let your requests be made known to God. And the peace of God, which surpasses all comprehension, will guard your hearts and your minds in Christ Jesus."
—Philippians 4:6–7 (the author's Combat Verse)

Note to the reader: If you haven't selected your "Life Verse" yet, consider doing it soon, with God's help!

"Therefore you are to be perfect, as your heavenly Father is perfect" (Matt. 5:48). Some have said that the word "perfect" means "mature." Either way, we humans are to strive to be, with the Holy Spirit's help, solidly mature and perfect, lacking nothing with which to serve our God in this life. We are to be perfected by time, natural growth, and the Holy Spirit into one who is competent to manage his own affairs and, over time, to offer the mature counsel of God-shaped experience to others when asked. Which reminds me of a humorous saying that I heard many years ago: "If experience is the name given to our mistakes, then most of us have a huge amount of experience." I sure have!

Talking about mistakes, let's take a look at God's view of today's so-called "Social Issues." Many teens and twenties I've talked with have no solid biblical knowledge about these things, things like adultery, abortion, homosexuality, etc. If I am to be fair to you, I must inform you about these so that you will know, and be able to lead, as a good Shepherd, in telling others about these truths from God's Word, when it comes up in your own discussions.

The following definitions are from "The Christian Broadcasting Network Counseling Ministry Handbook," 1985, 209:

> Immorality: moral behavior contrary to God's standards.
>
> Perversion: turning from the true and/or proper purpose of sexual intercourse; misusing or abusing it, such as homosexuality (includes lesbianism), sadism, masochism, and transvestitism (we add pedophilia).
>
> Adultery: sexual intercourse with a person other than your spouse.
>
> Fornication: illicit sexual intercourse when you aren't married.

Sexual sins are committed because of lust (I John 2:16; Gal. 5:19–21). When you allow improper sexual drives to control you as a Christian, an inner tension will result in your mind, emotions, and will. You will want to be spiritual, but find yourself being a slave to sensuality. The result is double-mindedness (James 1:8), leading to a reprobate mind (Romans 1:28).

The following list of Bible references is provided to help your research to vividly show what our God has to say about such issues. The world's view of them is at odds with what God, our Creator, has to say about them—no surprise. There is an old saying, "Watch out if you're in step with the world, because the world has never been in step with God."

My hope and prayer is that this will help you see the truth—His Truth—and live accordingly. And if anyone wants to argue with you about any of these, simply tell them, "These are God's rules, not mine; I'm just the messenger." You could also remind them that God's standard in behaviors is for our own good. He wants none of us to remain in sin; He wants us all to receive His Salvation by Grace as we discussed in the chapter "Be Surrendered."

Abortion: Exodus 20:13; Deuteronomy 5:17; Psalm 139:13–16; Isaiah 49:1b, 5a; Jeremiah 1:5a

Addictions: Proverbs 20:1; Proverbs 21:17; Proverbs 23:20–21, 29–35; Isaiah 5:11, 12, 22; Hosea 4:11; 1 Corinthians 5:11; 1 Corinthians 6:9; Galatians 5:19–21; 1 John 3:8

Adultery: Exodus 20:14; Proverbs 2:16–19; Proverbs 6:20–29; Proverbs 9:13–18; Matthew 5:28; Romans 13:14; 1 Corinthians 6:9–10, 13–20; 1 Thessalonians 4:3–7; Hebrews 13:4

Homosexuality: Genesis 19:4–7, 22–26; Leviticus 18:22, 20:13; Romans 1:18, 24, 26, 27, 28; 1 Corinthians 6:9–10; 1 Timothy 1:9–11

Incest/Molestation: Leviticus 18:6, 29; Leviticus 20:11–12, 14, 17; Mark 6:18; 1 Corinthians 5:1, 5; 1 Corinthians 6:9–10, 13–20; 1 Corinthians 7:2; 1 Thessalonians 4:3–6

Lust: Matthew 5:28; Romans 6:12; Galatians 5:16–21; Titus 2:11–12; 1 John 2:15–16

Marriage/Divorce: Genesis 2:18–24; Proverbs 18:22; Matthew 5:32; Matthew 19:3–9; Mark 10:9; Romans 7:2; 1 Corinthians 7:2–4, 10–16; Ephesians 5:31; 1 Timothy 5:14; Hebrews 13:4; Note: God has made it plain that marriage is between one man and one woman. So using the term "marriage" to describe a same-gender union mocks God (Gal. 6:7). Calling an antelope a kangaroo does not make it a kangaroo, just as calling a homosexual union a marriage does not make it so—it is still a lie straight from the pit of Hell!

Suicide (Self-Inflicted Murder): Exodus 20:13; Psalm 40:1–3a; John 10:10; Philippians 4:6–8, 19

Temptation: Matthew 26:41; Romans 6:23; 1 Corinthians 10:13; Galatians 5:19–23; Galatians 6:7–8; Hebrews 2:18; James 1:2–3, 12–16

There is another element of our culture that, for the most part, has "gone south." That is the entertainment industry. Because of the worldwide reach of the mostly horrific outputs from TV and film, the US has the dubious distinction of having infected other peoples with our alleged craving for sex, violence, filthy language, and worse. Syndicated weekly columnist Peggy Noonan says this in an article entitled "Declarations—The Dark Night Rises":

> A particularly devilish injustice is that many of the wealthy men and women of the filmmaking industry go to great lengths to protect their own children from the products they make . . . They don't want them watching that garbage . . . Our culture, [parents] know, is their foe. The culture brings sick

into the room. They have to guard against it, be hyper vigilant . . . (Noonan 2012)

So you must be vigilant for yourself and later for your own children. There are increasing amounts of generally good movies available; I speak of some of them at the end of "Looking Ahead." With careful selection, you can find decent TV fare as well.

There will be times when you are attacked by the enemy of your soul, the devil. Use James 4:7b against him: "Resist the devil and he will flee from you." And yes, I have told you of this important verse earlier in the book, but it is such a terrific weapon for us to use against the devil that it bears repeating here. And do not forget that the first part of that verse calls us to "Submit therefore to God."

Never be afraid to fail. Think carefully through your planned path ahead and then, if you believe it is a worthy objective and you can do it with God's help, do it with all the gusto you can muster, holding nothing back. If you succeed, the victory is heady and prepares you for the next great victory with Him. If you fail, it will not be because of a faint heart—and it will steel and toughen you for the next great venture. President Abraham Lincoln, one of America's great presidents, failed many, many times before finally achieving his goal of president of the United States of America. And thereafter, he served his country with transcendent distinction and a steely resolve to do well as God gave him insight.

A man named Ron Chernow has written a biography (*Washington: A Life*) recently about our first president, the "Father of our Country," George Washington. Chernow says, "What Washington's life shows is the importance of clarity of vision, of tenacity of purpose and character, and how much can be accomplished in life if you keep your sights set on your ultimate goals."[8]

I have finished the work I believe God gave me here for you, your dad, mom, or mentor. I credit God for any good for you in this book. He has pulled out of me from my long experience in this life the true essences of what you need to embrace and make your own. If you weave all I have shared with you here deep into who you are and who you become, you will have become a man of whom the world is not worthy. You will have Become a Man of Integrity and Godly Character—a Shepherd.

> *A righteous man who walks in his integrity—*
>
> *How blessed are his sons after him?*
>
> —Proverbs 20:7

---

[8] Ron Chernow, *Washington: A Life* (New York: The Penguin Press, 2010).

Bibliography

Cahn, Jonathan. *The Harbinger: The Ancient Mystery That Holds the Secret of America's Future.* Florida: Front Line, 2011.

Chernow, Ron. *Washington: A Life.* New York: Penguin Press, 2010.

McBride, Jim. *Rite of Passage: A Father's Blessing.* Chicago: Moody Publishers, 2001.

Noonan, Peggy. "Declarations: The Dark Night Rises." *Wall Street Journal*, Sunday edition, sec. A17, July 28, 2012.

Suggested Reading, Annotated

Getz, Gene A. *The Measure of a Man.* Glendale, California: Regal Books div. of G/L Pubs, 1974.
Discusses each requirement for an Elder/Deacon.

Harris, Alex and Brett Harris. *Do Hard Things: A Teenage Rebellion Against Low Expectations.* Multnomah, 2008.
This is a book (another has already been written) by two Christian teens who have been raised by Godly parents to stand strong (1 Cor. 16:13–14) for Christ in the marketplace of ideas and everyday living. They give solid advice and exhortation to live above the common level of life and matter for God. This book should be in every young man's library and have well-worn pages.

Hughes, R. Kent. *Disciplines of a Godly Man.* Illinois: Crossway Books, 1991.
One of the very best books for mentoring men. Covers it all from a fully scriptural point of view. Subjects include purity, marriage, fatherhood, friendship, elements of the soul (mind, devotion, prayer, worship), integrity, the tongue, work, elements of ministry (church, leadership, giving, witness), through to the grace of discipline. This book should be in every Christian man's library.

Lewis, Dr. Robert. www.mensfraternity.com. This website is all about "authentic manhood," about becoming the man you've always wanted to be. The site offers several excellent group and individual study series. I recommend this highly.

Marrella, Len. *In Search of Ethics—Conversations with Men and Women of Character.* Florida: DC Press, 2001.
Covers the moral environment, business and ethics, honor, idealism, sacrifice, values, character, integrity, truth, responsibility, humility, etc.

Morley, Patrick. *The Man in the Mirror (Solving the 24 Problems Men Face).* Michigan: Zondervan Publishing House, 1997.
Talks about solving our "man" problems of identity, relationship, money, time, temperament, integrity, and changing to be better.

Morley, Patrick. *Ten Secrets for the Man in the Mirror.* Michigan: Zondervan, 2000.
Talks about lordship, balance, vocation, suffering, discipleship, stewardship, witnessing, service, humor, and love.

Ruark, Robert. *The Old Man and The Boy.* Henry Holt and Company, 1957. Owl Books, 1993.
This timeless classic tells the story of a remarkable friendship between a young boy and his grandfather. It is a heartwarming, eloquent, and ultimately poignant tale

about choices, about responsibility, and about becoming a man.

Stinson, Randy and Dan Dumas. *A Guide to Biblical Manhood.* Southern Baptist Theological Seminary, SBTS Press, 2011.

A great little book of 109 pages in four sections: Lessons in Manhood, A Godly Husband, A Godly Father, and A Pastor's Guide.

Weber, Stu. *Tender Warrior—God's Intention for a Man.* Multnomah Books, 1993.

Talks about facing yourself, the four pillars of manhood, staying power, a man and his wife, his children, his God, his friends, a man and his leadership, etc.

Wiersbe, Warren W. *Be a Real Teen.* Moody Press, 1965.

The best 127-page read for teens who want to truly be a super teen. Topics cover things like relax and enjoy being a teen, it's okay to dream, preparing for your future, how to fail, how far can I go, how can God work in my heart, etc.

Study Guide

The purpose of this study guide or reader's questionnaire is to enhance the reader's understanding of the concepts discussed in the book. With serious attention, it will help you "lock in" the foundational truths of mature, manly behavior. It can help launch you well down the road toward becoming a Man of Integrity and Godly Character.

The study guide will assist both readers and teachers of the book. It is organized by chapter with questions designed to create thoughtful contemplation and/or discussion. Where appropriate, a question is followed by page number(s) in parentheses to indicate where the proper response may be found. There is one basic question that you should ask yourself of each of the twelve Behaviors: "Why is this Behavior a critical building block to my becoming a Man of Integrity and Godly Character?"

The author wants you to study your way through this book with your dad, your mom, or an adult male mentor. These Behaviors will mean much more to you if you explore them with someone older who has been through the bumps of life. We all do better at anything if we learn it from someone who has been there and done it successfully, or even unsuccessfully. But you must bring a teachable spirit with you to this endeavor.

As you, a parent or mentor, walk your son or mentee through the book, your own experience should spark additional questions as you go. Use examples from your own experience to illustrate and to further explain and define the Behavior being studied. You might also read some of the source materials listed in Suggested Reading to help you help your young man become that Man of Integrity and Godly Character.

As to the one transaction discussed in detail in the chapter "Be Surrendered," you, the reader, may want advice and counsel from your Christian dad or mom, or the minister of a local, Christ-centered, Bible-teaching church.

If you are only now arriving at this section and have already worked your way through the book on your own, it will not hurt you to do it again, only this time, do it with your dad, mom, or adult male mentor. In fact, doing it again with someone older and more experienced will help you correct any misconceptions you may have developed on your own, and it will help lock in all the good that is here for you—for life.

PREFACE

1. Do you think the author's many years of experience working with soldiers in their late teens and early twenties qualifies him to write to you about these topics?

2. Do you think the author has a deep desire to see our nation turned around to become again the great nation it once was?

3. Do you think he wants you to become an important part of that grand vision for rescuing the nation?

4. Do you see yourself becoming part of that grand vision, and do you see the teachings of this book being the vehicle by which you can become a leader in that great endeavor?

5. Do you thoroughly understand the two diagrams and their captions? Could you explain them to someone else with confidence?

FIRST THINGS FIRST

1. Talk about the pro and con implications of Proverbs 22:6. (2)

2. What does being a man for God mean to you? (3)

3. Read Matthew 12:34b and Proverbs 4:23. What do these two scriptures say about your heart? (3)

4. What makes you who you are? (3)

5. How do you define a person's heart? (3)

6. Let's talk about integrity (3) . . . then character. (4)

7. How is Godly Character different from character? (4)

8. Why is moral courage an essential part of a man's character? (4–5)

9. Have you firmed up your dream of who you want to be and what you want to do?

BE SURRENDERED

1. Being surrendered means being saved. From what are you saved? (8)

2. Can you state in your own words why each of us needs to be saved? (8)

3. Why is becoming a Christian important to us as men (aside from the obvious benefit of being with God for eternity)? (7)

4. Have you a question about the story of man's fall and redemption? (7–11)

5. Pages 9 and 10 tell you how to become a Christian. If you wish to pray to receive Christ, you can do this yourself, or you might want to ask a Christian adult (mother, father, pastor, or teacher) to help you. If you have taken this step, write down your brief story about this experience. This becomes your personal story portion when you share the Good News of Jesus Christ with others.

6. Name two things you should do in addition to sharing your story of becoming a Christian. (10)

BE DISCIPLINED

1. What do you think of when you hear the word "discipline"?

2. Does discipline come easily to us? Why? (13–14)

3. What is the difference between self-discipline and imposed discipline?

4. Training and practice are required to become a mature self-disciplined man. On a scale of 1–10, 10 being excellent, how would you rate your maturity in the following?

   Purity   Sober   Outlook   Focused
   Committed   Self-Starter   Physical Condition
   Other Areas

5. On any category where you rated yourself less than 9, what steps will you take to improve? What else will you do to become more disciplined?

6. Why is sexual purity so hard for young men (and young women) today? (14–15)

7. Why are persistence and determination important?

BE ENCOURAGING

1. What is so special about an encourager? (21)

2. Name two or three characteristics that most encouragers have. (21)

3. Are you an encourager or a *dis*courager? What can you do to become a better encourager? (22)

4. Who do you go to when you feel discouraged or defeated?

5. Explain why being an encourager is a key part of being a leader, a Shepherd.

BE FORGIVING

1. Did you have difficulty "accepting" all of the aspects of "forgiving" as defined on page 25? If so, which one(s)? Let's talk it through. (25)

2. Why is holding grudges (unforgiveness) bad for us personally, as well as for the relationship? (26–27)

3. What do you think is the "big issue" in our being unable to forgive fully? (25, 27, 28)

4. What do you think the so-called Golden Rule has to say about forgiving? (28)

5. What is the relationship between forgiveness and love? John 3:16 (26)

6. What are you going to do to be more forgiving?

BE GENTLE

1. You may not think of a man being gentle, yet the most powerful being ever on earth, Jesus, is the one saying "blessed are the gentle" (meek). What does gentle mean then?

2. As a gentle man, what are you to do if someone mocks you or your faith—or wants to belittle you? (Prov. 15:1)

3. Does being gentle suggest to you someone who is not arrogant, who does not think of himself too highly, who is genuinely at ease with all others around him, who really sees us all as equal before our great God? In short, could you say a gentle man is a humble man?

4. How are you going to work toward becoming gentler?

BE HONORABLE

1. Explain "honorable." Describe a man of honor. (33)

2. Who, in your view, is honorable? Does his example influence you? How?

3. Name three or four things a man of honor practices. (34)

4. Describe a dishonorable man. (34)

5. Why is it that most people want to deal with honorable men? (36)

6. Why is being honorable so fragile? (36–37)

7. Explain the relationship of morality to ethics and to being honorable. (37)

8. Where can you find a code of right and wrong?

9. What did General Creighton Abrams say about honor? (36)

10. What are you going to do to Be Honorable?

BE INVOLVED

1. Why is being involved (at home, at school, at work, at church) a sign of your maturing? (39–40)

2. The following is a partial list of activities and responsibilities of young people. List the ones in which you are presently involved.

   Home Chores (make bed, mow lawn, clean bedroom, wash cars, other)

   School (athletics, clubs, music, drama, other)

   Church (youth group, volunteer at a ministry for elderly, serve in VBS, food pantry, other)

   Job (do I just do minimum required or do I look for ways to help the company?)

   Friends (do I influence others for God and good?)

3. While on earth, Jesus was an example of someone who served others through teaching, friendships, feeding people, and sharing God's message. From your activity list above, how could you use these activities to serve others?

4. Why is associating with older men, especially in the church, a significant help toward maturing as a man? (40–41)

5. What areas of Romans 12:9–13 do you have trouble applying in your life? (41)

6. Describe why being involved in many aspects of your life while a young man can help you select your life's direction.

7. What are some areas or ways in which you have decided to become more involved? (42)

BE KNOWLEDGEABLE

1. What are some necessary personal "ingredients" to becoming knowledgeable? (44–45)

2. Why is book reading essential to gaining knowledge? (45)

3. How do you put the "Godly" in a Godly man? (46)

4. What does King Solomon call men who hate knowledge? (Prov. 1:22, Prov. 13:16)

5. How does managing your time contribute to your knowledge? (45)

6. Why is being knowledgeable a lifelong pursuit? (46–47)

7. We can *know* a lot of things. What is needed to make that knowledge useful?

8. Why does being a Shepherd—a leader—require you to be very knowledgeable? (44)

9. Set three goals for yourself to increase your knowledge and its application.

BE MERCIFUL

1. Explain mercy. (49)

2. Compassion fuels mercy. Do you remember a time when your compassion for someone resulted in your being merciful to them?

3. What aspects of Romans 12:14–21 cause you concern? (50)

4. How would you describe your usual or normal attitude toward those less fortunate than you? (51)

5. What does the writer in Romans 12:21 say will be the outcome if we practice these commands?

6. What are you going to do to become more merciful?

BE PRAYERFUL

1. Describe prayer. (53)

2. Why do we pray? (53–54)

3. Do you pray? If so, what do you usually pray about? (53–54)

4. Why is prayer essential and important? (54–55)

5. From page 55 fill in the chart below:

BODY	SPIRIT
1.	1.
2.	2.
3.	3.

6. Summarize the last paragraph on page 55.

7. Explain the importance of having a prayer partner. (56)

8. Why should we pray to God daily? (56)

9. What are you going to do to be more prayerful? And is that a promise to you or to God?

BE RESPECTFUL

1. Were you taught as a child to be respectful, especially of adults? If so, how were you to show such respect?

2. Why should you be respectful of others? (59)

3. What does being disrespectful to others reveal about you? (60–61)

4. Can you think of areas other than slovenly dress, bad language, late to meetings, that show disrespect to others?

5. What does the Bible say about respecting your parents? (Exod. 20:12)

6. Are there some changes you need to make in attitude and behavior to become more respectful to others?

BE RESPONSIBLE

1. How do you think you stack up against the full definition for responsible? (65) What specifically will you do about it?

2. What does the Bible teach about responsibility and work? (2 Thess. 3:10b, Prov. 22:29)

3. What kind of man do you want to be? (See top paragraph of page 66)

4. What is the most satisfying part of life for a real man? (66)

5. Many employers complain they cannot find dependable workers. In what ways can a man show he is a dependable (responsible) worker?

6. What part does lying or not lying play in being responsible? (67)

7. Why is managing your personal affairs according to the Bible an important element of being responsible? (68)

BE TOUGH MINDED

1. Why is it important to think with your head and not your heart? (69)

2. How does being tough minded relate to:
   a. Right decisions when it means parting with your friends' choices? (69–70)
   b. Becoming a leader (Shepherd)? (70)

3. Explain how you can be tough but gentle at the same time. (69)

4. Explain the difference between resilience and weakness. (69)

5. What does "be comfortable in your own skin" mean to you?

6. What are four or five personal characteristics of a good leader? (70–71)

7. What are you going to do to improve your own tough-mindedness?

LOOKING AHEAD

1. Why is it wise to seek the advice and counsel of someone who has been through what you are considering doing?

2. Name two important principles under the heading Work. (73)

3. Explain why you believe it is wise to get more training (or education) before entering the work world.

4. Higher education requires time and sacrifice. Name some things that **must** be sacrificed while you are in school.

5. Explain why debt can ruin your financial future.

6. Why is it important to get out of your parents' home when you become an adult?

7. How does being on the "same page" in your faith, finances, interests, children, etc., affect a decision to marry? (77–80)

8. Why must a husband think long and hard about becoming a father *before* children are born? (80–83)

9. On pages 80 through 83, the author discusses fatherhood and its responsibilities. Discuss each of the following:

    a. A dad's job is to raise adults.

    b. Dad must be the spiritual leader of his home.

    c. God has a plan for each member of the home.

10. What is the single most important task a Christian is given to accomplish? (83)

11. According to Jonathon Cahn, America has traded God for idols. Name five of these idols. (84–85)

12. Have you made your decision as Joshua did (Joshua 24:14–15): "as for me and my house, we will serve the Lord"? That one decision will affect everything you do in life.

13. In thinking about your life's dream or your life's direction, have you considered running for public office? This nation needs good and godly men of integrity and character and great courage to enter the political contests for public office. The only way the evil of the day can turn around is for Men of Integrity and Godly Character to successfully run for office. We need such men to become our next leaders—our next Shepherds.

*How blessed is the man who finds wisdom
And the man who gains understanding . . .
Long life is in her [wisdom's] right hand,
In her left hand are riches and honor.*

—Proverbs 3:13,16

About the Author

Thomas B. McDonald III, the son of a military father, entered the military through the US Military Academy at West Point, New York. After graduation he completed training as a paratrooper and ranger, and settled into his military specialty as a communicator. He commanded a battalion and a brigade, a total of some 3,700 soldiers, mostly young men. Retiring as a colonel after twenty-six years of service, he entered the business world. After three years, he formed and ran his own company for nine years, retiring a second time in 1996.

While attending the Army War College, Tom gave his life to Jesus Christ in 1976. This decision had a profound impact on his life. It helped inspire him to write this, his first book, after observing the need—in business, government, academia, the church, and the military—for more Men of Integrity and Godly Character.

Tom and his wife, Kay, live near Atlanta, Georgia. They enjoy traveling the world and serving people through their church. Tom enjoys time with family and friends, and teaching the Bible.